STEAMBOATS

IN

ICE

STEAMBOATS IN ICE
1872

More True Stories About Shipwreck
And Other Historical Events
During One Incredible Year
On the Great Lakes

Volume 2

By James Donahue

Anchor Publications
Cass City, Mich.
1995

Copyright by James Donahue
All Rights Reserved

First Edition, 1995
Anchor Publications
P. O. Box 34, Cass City, Mich. 48726

Printed in the United States of America. No part of this book may be reproduced in any manner whatsoever without written permission except in the case of brief quotations embodied in critical articles and reviews.

ISBN 0-9626947-3-8

About the Cover Photo

The steamer *State of Michigan* stands locked in ice on Lake Michigan, about a mile from shore and the safe confines of the Manitowoc, Wisconsin harbor in March, 1885. The steamer, a contemporary of 1872, escaped the ice that winter.

About the Title

The title for this book, Steamboats In Ice, reflects true events. The year 1872 began with steamboats battling massive ice jams. The shipping season ended abruptly with a killer November storm that trapped a number of boats on the lower end of Lake Superior and on Mud Lake, the route from the St. Marys River into Lake Huron.

Contents

List of Illustrations
Introduction page 1

The Spring Thaw
Ice, page 7
Tugboat Fire, page 8
Thawing Out the *Goble,* page 9
Racing the Ice, page 10
Wrecked at the Pier, page 11
Fighting Death in a Small Boat, page 12
A Gallant Rescue, page 13
More Trouble With Ice, page 14
Wreck of the *Eva Cone,* page 15
Steamboats In Ice, page 16
Schooner Upside Down, page 18
The Copper Strike, page 19
Ramming Through the Straits, page 21
Collision at Marblehead, page 23
The *Somerset* Wreck, page 24
The *Compound* Explosion, page 24
Saving the *Chicago,* page 27
More Ice Casualties, page 29
New Era of Shipping, page 30
For Safer Waters, page 31
The *Marquette* Miracle, page 32
Strange Sinking of the *Fulton,* page 34
Collision in the Fog, page 34
Bad Night for the *Josephine,* page 36
The Wreckers, page 36

Summertime Troubles
Fire on the *Dove,* page 45
Saving the *Giant,* page 45
Hogged Out, page 46
The *Ransom* Affair, page 47
Remembering the *Maine,* page 48
Dragging On the Bottom, page 49
Union Trouble, page 52
The Burning *Kingston,* page 53
Strange Tides, page 55
Aboard the *Sweepstakes,* page 56
Launching the *Montana,* page 56
The Waterspout, page 58
Power Boats on the Erie Canal, page 59
Smoking in Bed, page 63
Suprise Shipwreck, page 64

The *Manitoba's* Bad Luck, page 65
Burning of Alpena, page 66
Death Blow at Buffalo, page 67
Death Fight at Cleveland, page 68
The Big Hauls, page 68
Fire Aboard the *Champion,* page 71
Loss of the *D. L. Couch,* page 72
The *Black Duck,* page 72
Burning of the *Mary Robinson,* page 73
The Old Steamer Burns, page 74
Fearless Frenzy, page 74
Sinking a Burning Tug, page 75
A Sitting Duck, page 76
Killed by Lightning, page 77
Lake Breeze Fire, page 78
Fire on the *Bertschy,* page 79
"Oh Lord, Have Mercy..." page 79
Stuck in the Mud, page 81
Late Summer Blow, page 82
Gospel Ship, page 84

Storms of Autumn
They Lost Their Nerve, page 91
The *Sargent* is Missing! page 92
Where There is Smoke... page 93
Striking for a Better Way, page 93
Erie Horror Story, page 94
Burning *Bemis,* page 96
Saving the *W. H. Hawkins,* page 97
Riding in on a Wheelhouse, page 97
Other Storm Casualties, page 99
Capsized, page 100
Burning of *Dalhousie,* page 101
September Death Gale, page 102
Wreck of the *Galena,* page 102
Wreck of the *Iron City,* page 105
Aboard the *Phil Sheridan,* page 107
Wreck of the *John H. Drake,* page 107
Strange Case of the *G. J. Whitney,* page 108
The *Corsair* Saga, page 108
Collision in the Storm, page 112
Wreck of the *York State,* page 113
Blown Backwards, page 113
Slamming into Logs, page 114
Surviving the Storm, page 115
Lost Lumber Barges 1, page 116
Lost Lumber Barges 2, page 117
Lost Lumber Barges 3, page 118
Lumber Hookers Aground, page 119
The *Montezuma,* page 120

The Unwanted Corpse, page 121
Other Gale Casualties, page 122
Wreck of the *B. R. Lummis,* page 126
Bill Angell's Big Mistake, page 127
Burning *China,* page 128
Wreck of the *Lac La Belle,* page 128
Murder at the Welland Canal, page 133
Alaska on the Rocks, page 133
Blown to Atoms, page 135
Where is the *Eliza Williams?* page 135

The Ice Returns
The Mate and How Many? page 139
Drifting Sailors, page 140
Saving the *Cleveland,* page 140
Sinking of the *Forest Queen,* page 141
The Boston Fire, page 142
Wreck of the *Willis,* page 144
Ship Full of Peas, page 144
Wild Times at Duluth, page 145
The Storm at Marquette, page 146
Burning of the *John Stewart,* page 147
Wreck of the *New Hampshire,* page 148
Sinking of the *Minot Mitchell,* page 148
Wreck of the *Mary Ward,* page 149
An Old Relic Burns, page 151
Jupiter and *Saturn,* page 151
Close Call for the *Middlesex,* page 154
Rescue at Erie, page 154
Bad Times for the *Burlington,* page 155
Joyful Survival, page 156
A Man and a Boy, page 157
More Lost Barges, page 158
Other Casualties, page 159
Sailors on Snowshoes, page 161
Broken Rudder, page 164
Fighting Ice and Snow, page 165
Back and Forth Across Lake Michigan, page 166
One Last Try, page 168

Summing Up
Other Wrecks of 1872, page 171
A Dangerous Profession, page 172
The Final Counting, page 176
Bibliography, page 177
Index of Ships, page 179
Glossery of Nautical Terms, page 192
About the Author, page 194

List of Illustrations

Alaska, str., p 134, photo courtesy Institute for Great Lakes Research, Perrysburg, Ohio
Atlantic, str., p 147, photo courtesy Institute for Great Lakes Research, Perrysburg, Ohio
Balize, tug, p 47, photo courtesy Institute for Great Lakes Research, Perrysburg, Ohio
Bemis, Philo S., tug, p 96, photo courtesy Institute for Great Lakes Research, Perrysburg, Ohio
Benton, prop., p 164, photo from Beeson's Marine Directory, 1900, courtesy Institute for Great Lakes Research, Perrysburg, Ohio
Bundy, Capt. Henry, p 84, photo courtesy Institute for Great Lakes Research, Perrysburg, Ohio
Burcher Boy, sch., p 125, photo courtesy Institute for Great Lakes Research, Perrysburg, Ohio
Burlington, prop., p 156, photo courtesy Institute for Great Lakes Research, Perrysburg, Ohio
Canal barges and lake schooner on Erie Canal Basin, Buffalo, New York, p 61, drawing from Louden G. Wilson Collection, Institute for Great Lakes Research, Perrysburg, Ohio
Canisteo, str., p 67, photo courtesy Institute for Great Lakes Research, Perrysburg, Ohio
Champion, tug., p 71, drawing courtesy Institute for Great Lakes Research, Perrysburg, Ohio
Champion with barges in tow, tug, p 69, painting courtesy Institute for Great Lakes Research, Perrysburg, Ohio.
Chicago, prop., p 27, photo courtesy Wilson Collection, Institute for Great Lakes Research, Perrysburg, Ohio
City of Boston, str., p 111, picture courtesy Institute for Great Lakes Research, Perrysburg, Ohio
Cooke, Jay, str., p 114, photo courtesy Institute for Great Lakes Research, Perrysburg, Ohio.
Corning, Erastus, sch. p 104, picture of painting courtesy Institute for Great Lakes Research, Perrysburg, Ohio
Crawford, R. C., sch., p 91, photo courtesy Institute for Great Lakes Research, Perrysburg, Ohio
Cuba, prop., p 31, photo courtesy Institute for Great Lakes Research, Perrysburg, Ohio
Danforth, F. L., tug, p 75, photo courtesy Institute for Great Lakes Research, Perrysburg, Ohio.
Day Spring, sch., p 77, photo courtesy Institute for Great Lakes Research, Perrysburg, Ohio

Detroit, prop., p 119, artist's drawing courtesy Institute for Great Lakes Research, Perrysburg, Ohio

Dix, John A., str., p 152, photo courtesy Institute for Great Lakes Research, Perrysburg, Ohio

Dormer, Grace, str., p 63, photo courtesy Institute for Great Lakes Research, Perrysburg, Ohio

Favorite, tug, 0, photo courtesy Insitute for Great Lakes Research, Perrysburg, Ohio

Fisk, James Jr., str., p 165, photo courtesy Institute for Great Lakes Research, Perrysburg, Ohio

Forest Queen, str., p 142, photo courtesy Institute for Great Lakes Research, Perrysburg, Ohio

Gladiator, tug, p 70, photo courtesy Institute for Great Lakes Research, Perrysburg, Ohio

Glad Tidings, sch., p 87, photo courtesy Institute for Great Lakes Research, Perrysburg, Ohio

Graham, Jennie, sch., p 19, artist's drawing courtesy Louden G. Wilson Collection, Institute for Great Lakes Research, Perrysburg, Ohio

Grain terminals and harbor scene at Buffalo, New York, p 191, artist's drawing from Louden G. Wilson Collection, Institute for Great Lakes Research, Perrysburg, Ohio.

Granite State, prop., p 23, drawing courtesy Milwaukee Public Library, Milwaukee, Wisconsin.

Kingston, str., p 54, photo courtesy Institute for Great Lakes Research, Perrysburg, Ohio

Lac La Belle, prop., p 129, photo courtesy Institute for Great Lakes Research, Perrysburg, Ohio

Lake Michigan, str., p 121, photo courtesy Institute for Great Lakes Research, Perrysburg, Ohio

Lawrence, str., p 16, photo courtesy Institute for Great Lakes Research, Perrysburg, Ohio

Leviathan, wrecking tug., p 39, photo courtesy Institute for Great Lakes Research, Perrysburg, Ohio

Marquette, sch., p 33, photo courtesy Institute for Great Lakes Research, Perrysburg, Ohio

Manistee, prop., p 7, photo courtesy Institute for Great Lakes Research, Perrysburg, Ohio

Montana, prop., p 57, photo courtesy Institute for Great Lakes Research, Perrysburg, Ohio

Manitoba, str., p 65, photo courtesy Institute for Great Lakes Research, Perrysburg, Ohio

Merchant, prop., p 40, drawing courtesy Institute for Great Lakes Research, Perrysburg, Ohio.

Detroit, prop., p 119, artist's drawing courtesy Institute for Great Lakes Research, Perrysburg, Ohio

Dix, John A., str., p 152, photo courtesy Institute for Great Lakes Research, Perrysburg, Ohio

Dormer, Grace, str., p 63, photo courtesy Institute for Great Lakes Research, Perrysburg, Ohio

Favorite, tug, 0, photo courtesy Insitute for Great Lakes Research, Perrysburg, Ohio

Fisk, James Jr., str., p 165, photo courtesy Institute for Great Lakes Research, Perrysburg, Ohio

Forest Queen, str., p 142, photo courtesy Institute for Great Lakes Research, Perrysburg, Ohio

Gladiator, tug, p 70, photo courtesy Institute for Great Lakes Research, Perrysburg, Ohio

Glad Tidings, sch., p 87, photo courtesy Institute for Great Lakes Research, Perrysburg, Ohio

Graham, Jennie, sch., p 19, artist's drawing courtesy Louden G. Wilson Collection, Institute for Great Lakes Research, Perrysburg, Ohio

Grain terminals and harbor scene at Buffalo, New York, p 191, artist's drawing from Louden G. Wilson Collection, Institute for Great Lakes Research, Perrysburg, Ohio.

Granite State, prop., p 23, drawing courtesy Milwaukee Public Library, Milwaukee, Wisconsin.

Kingston, str., p 54, photo courtesy Institute for Great Lakes Research, Perrysburg, Ohio

Lac La Belle, prop., p 129, photo courtesy Institute for Great Lakes Research, Perrysburg, Ohio

Lake Michigan, str., p 121, photo courtesy Institute for Great Lakes Research, Perrysburg, Ohio

Lawrence, str., p 16, photo courtesy Institute for Great Lakes Research, Perrysburg, Ohio

Leviathan, wrecking tug., p 39, photo courtesy Institute for Great Lakes Research, Perrysburg, Ohio

Marquette, sch., p 33, photo courtesy Institute for Great Lakes Research, Perrysburg, Ohio

Manistee, prop., p 7, photo courtesy Institute for Great Lakes Research, Perrysburg, Ohio

Manitoba, str., p 65, photo courtesy Institute for Great Lakes Research, Perrysburg, Ohio

Merchant, prop., p 40, drawing courtesy Institute for Great Lakes Research, Perrysburg, Ohio.

Messenger, prop., p 12, photo courtesy Institute for Great Lakes Research, Perrysburg, Ohio

Montana, prop., p 56, photo courtesy Institute for Great Lakes Research, Perrysburg, Ohio

Prindlville, John, wrecking str., p 22, photo courtesy Institute for Great Lakes Research, Perrysburg, Ohio

St. Albans, str., p 167, photo courtesy Institute for Great Lakes Research, Perrysburg, Ohio

St. Paul, str., p 162, photo courtesy Institute for Great Lakes Research, Perrysburg, Ohio

Torrent, tug, p 159, photo courtesy Institute for Great Lakes Research, Perrysburg, Ohio

Union, prop., p 53, photo courtesy Institute for Great Lakes Research, Perrysburg, Ohio.

Vanderbilt, prop., p 51, photo courtesy Institute for Great Lakes Research, Perrysburg, Ohio

Ward, Mary, str., p 149, artist's drawing courtesy Institute for Great Lakes Research, Perrysburg, Ohio

Wenona, prop., p 15, photo courtesy Institute for Great Lakes Research, Perrysburg, Ohio

Winslow, wrecking tug, p 37, photo courtesy Institute for Great Lakes Research, Perrysburg, Ohio

Acknowledgments:

Special thanks to the following people who helped in the research of this book: Robert W. Graham, archivist, Jay Martin, assistant archivist, and secretary Susan Riggs, of the Institute for Great Lakes Research, Perrysburg, Ohio; Harriet Eagle, head librarian, and assistant Jackie Graves, Sandusky Public Library; Patricia M. Virgil, assistant librarian, Buffalo and Erie County Historical Society, Buffalo, New York; May N. Stone, reference librarian, New York Historical Society, New York, N.Y.; and a number of unknown but helpful librarians at all ends of the Great Lakes, including the Milwaukee Public Library and Chicago Historical Society Library, who helped me dig through the dust of time.

Introduction

The five Great Lakes, all but one of them located between the boundaries of Canada and the United States, are the most unique fresh bodies of water in the world. Each lake is connected by some type of natural waterway, and each waterway is enhanced by man-made channels and locks, making it possible for large ships to travel the length and breadth of them. The Erie Canal, opened in 1825, linked the lakes to the Atlantic Ocean and world commerce. In more recent years, that link was improved via the St. Lawrence Seaway.

The men and women who maneuver ships through the lakes have developed skills very different from those of ocean sailors. Bringing a vessel across the Atlantic involves setting a course, then raising sails or running engines at full speed ahead. If all goes well, the ocean sailor expects to arrive at a destination in a few days. This is not the way it is done on the Great Lakes. One look at a map of the lakes shows why. Even though trips from Chicago to Buffalo, or possibly from Duluth to Kingston, can be as lengthy as an ocean trip in miles traveled, it never involves a simple course from one port to another. As the ships turn and twist their way through a complex series of obstacles, sailors always know that land, or more possibly a rocky reef, can be reached within a few hours and sometimes minutes if the vessel gets off course. The coastline is full of shallow shoals and unseen rock formations that can wreck any vessel that gets too close. More recent sonar mappings of the lake bottoms have exposed hidden dangers, like Lake Superior's Caribou Reef, a rock formation about twenty feet under the surface of the water that is thought to have torn the bottom out of numerous ships, including the Edmund Fitzgerald.

The task of locking a ship through the St. Marys River linking Lakes Huron and Superior, or the Welland Canal connecting Lakes Ontario and Erie, calls for special skills and sometimes long waits. There are so many tricks to bringing a vessel through the St. Clair and Detroit Rivers, connecting Lakes Huron and Erie, that professional pilots are required to bring foreign vessels through. These people, skilled in dealing with every sandbar and unseen current, board modern freighters at either end of the rivers and assume command until the ship reaches open water again.

In 1872, the year examined by this book, the demands on Great Lakes pilots were just as great, but not every pilot had the skills needed to stay out of trouble. The laws were much more lax, and there were so many boats of so many sizes, shapes and design, that shipwrecks were an everyday occurrence. They hit the rocks and sandbars. They ran into each other. They ran into piers and breakwaters. They exploded and caught fire. Sometimes they sank in storms. Many of the tragic events were unnecessary. The interests of shippers and ship owners sometimes overrode concerns for human life. The object too often was to move passengers and freight with little regard for the condition of the ship, or the skill of the operator. Every load moved from one port to another successfully meant money in somebody's pocket. The job of operating the boats was so dangerous that there was a fast turnover of staff. Sailors who stayed on consequently moved quickly up the ranks, sometimes taking command of ships long before they acquired the skills they needed to be good lake pilots. Ship owners dared to keep their vessels operating long after they were dangerously worn and ready to be retired. Many of the vessels that sank were wooden hulled vessels, sometimes stripped down steamers being used as barges tethered behind a steamer. They were so old and their hulls so rotted, they fell apart when caught in the stress of an autumn gale. The tragedy was that crews died with these derelict vessels.

This book, the second that examines shipping on the lakes during the decade of the 1870s, follows events has they happened in chronological order. Examination will show that shipping companies were so eager to run their boats, they put lives on the line by sending vessels out in the ice too early in the spring, and attempted to keep sending them out to carry freight after the ice closed the lakes to further traffic. The year 1872 was marked by severe winters at both ends of the shipping season. Great ice jams prevented early shipping in April and May, and a killer winter storm with subzero degree temperatures shut everything down again by December 1. The season also was filled with collisions, fires, sinkings and groundings. Extremely low water levels, caused from an abnormally dry period in 1871, hampered lumber operations and prevented ships from tieing up at many ports, including Chicago and Buffalo. Lighters often had to bring freight from the dock to the steamers, anchored offshore.

Please forgive the brevity of some of the stories. Sometimes, even though the wrecks might have claimed lives, the historical records were too thin for story development. Some of these wrecks are listed at the end of the book.

James Donahue

STEAMBOATS IN ICE

The Spring Thaw

March 1 - May 31

STEAMBOATS IN ICE

Propeller **Manistee** *blocked by ice on Lake Michigan. The ship attempted winter trips between Michigan and Wisconsin ports and was frequently caught in the ice. Courtesy Institute for Great Lakes Research*

Ice

The winter of 1871-72 was bitterly cold and brutal. The shipping season for 1871 ended with some vessels stranded in ice. Places like Lake Huron's Saginaw Bay, Georgian Bay, and the eastern end of Lake Erie became traps for lake captains who took chances; sailors who sought to expand their profits for the season with one last trip. Now, in March, as an armada of grain laden ships waited at Chicago for the ice to melt and the new shipping season to open, the reports of ice buildups along the route to Buffalo and beyond, were not encouraging. The ice at the Straits of Mackinac was thicker than usual. Vessels were not yet trying to find a way through it. Workers were still engaged in hauling lumber on horse-drawn sleds fifteen miles over the ice from the Manitou Islands in northern Lake Michigan, to the Michigan mainland. Few could recall when the lake was ever frozen between the islands and the mainland like that.

The Courier, Buffalo, New York, said that the ice in Lake Erie, just off the entrance to Buffalo harbor, measured twenty-six feet. Teams of horses were drawing lumber on the ice to Buffalo from Canada. The newspaper said Lake Erie seemed to be completely frozen over. Observers at Cleveland said on March 26 "there is an unbroken sheet of ice in the lake extending as far as the eye can see." The *Detroit Tribune* said Lake Huron's Saginaw Bay also was frozen over. The newspaper said a man walked across the ice that month from Charity Island to Au Gres River, Michigan, a distance of twenty-five miles.

Some ships were encountering ice at Michigan, Illinois and Wisconsin ports in southern Lake Michigan. The propeller *Manistee* got caught in ice and was driven aground near the breakwater at Grand Haven, Michigan. To get free, the crew lightened the ship by throwing off a deck load of cargo. That cargo included a hundred boxes of bacon, seventy-five barrels of pork, kegs of tobacco, a quantity of beer, rolls of leather and packages of dry goods.

Tugboat Fire

Amherstburg, Ontario
On the Detroit River
Saturday, March 1

The fire fighters of Amherstburg may have wondered if ship fires at the river were going to be routine harbingers of spring. One year earlier the steamer *Florence* burned at about this same time. Now yet another vessel was burning.

As the men and horses dashed in the night through the streets that night pulling a smoking steam pumper toward the blaze, they saw it was the faithful tugboat *M. I. Mills* that was afire. The blaze was sweeping the tug's wooden superstructure even as the pumper was rolled out of the barn.

Volunteer fire fighters and men of the community gathered in one united effort to save the *Mills*. They snuffed out the fire before it ruined the hull or engines. The damage was limited to the cabin and deck, which could be rebuilt by skilled carpenters and shipbuilders in a few weeks. Owner M. B. Kean said the damage was covered by insurance.

Thawing Out the *Goble*

On Southern Lake Huron
Near Port Huron, Michigan
Friday, April 12

The schooner *George Goble*, under the command of Capt. C. H. Meyers, looked bedraggled as it made its way slowly into the headwaters of the St. Clair River. As the tugboat *S. H. Martin* steamed out to meet it, the crew began to smell the rotting corn in the holds. They noticed the rips in the boat's neglected sails, saw the faded and tattered flag at its staff, and observed the melting ice still draping the hull. The paint was so worn along the hull that in some places, bare wood was visible. This was no ordinary ship arriving at Port Huron. The *Goble* was a lucky vessel, completing a voyage that started nearly six months earlier and got interrupted by a severe winter storm that left it locked in ice.

The *Goble's* troubles started on December 5, as the ship was sailing from Chicago to Buffalo with a load of corn. There are conflicting stories about what happened. One story in the *Port Huron Weekly Times* said the *Goble* grounded on a reef. Other accounts never mentioned a grounding. They said the ship got trapped in ice near Kettle Point, Ontario. When it became obvious that the *Goble* was stranded for the winter, the crew walked ashore. Captain Meyers and the first mate, a man named Haines, stayed aboard until the schooner worked its way free again. It turned out to be a long winter for the two men. They occasionally walked to shore and brought food and supplies with the help of a hand-pulled sled. At one point the stove broke and the men were unable to maintain a good fire until they walked to shore and brought back a new one. They also brought out a good supply of firewood. The trips to shore were always fraught with danger. The ship was sometimes caught in relatively stable ice, but at other times the ice became broken and shifted with the wind. Sometimes the ice pressed against the wooden hull with such force Meyers was sure the boat would not withstand the pressure.

The *Goble* lay most of the winter in a place about two miles off the Canadian coast, and about twenty-two miles north of Port Huron. The plight of the vessel was known to would-be salvagers ashore. The crew of the *Martin* made a gallant effort in January to rescue the ship from its ice trap. The men spent days cutting a route for the tug through the ice in the Black River. It is not known if the *Martin* got out on the lake. Whatever happened, the tug did not succeed in rescuing the stranded schooner.

It was on April 12 that the shifting and thawing ice finally freed the *Goble*. Captain Meyers and Haines raised sail and brought the ship safely into harbor, even as a serious spring storm was developing. The gale struck that night from the west and raged all the next day. Some thought that it was fierce enough that the *Goble* would not have survived it if the ship had spent another day on the lake.

Meyers' only quoted remark? He said he never wanted to do anything like that again.

Racing the Ice

On Lake Ontario
Off Oswego, New York
Saturday, April 13

The schooners *Mary Taylor* and *Antelope* were making a run for Oswego harbor, and the folks on shore were making bets. The sails of the two ships were seen that afternoon when they were still about five miles out and three miles from shore, both racing swiftly before a northerly wind. The crews of the schooners didn't know what the shore watchers knew, that the wind also was blowing a large block of drifting ice southward across the harbor entrance. The bets were made on whether the schooners or the ice would get there first. The ice won.

The *Mary Taylor*, with Captain Ewart at the helm, got within five hundred feet of the west pier before the ice brought it to a stop. The ship stayed there for five days until the tug *Major Dana* broke through and towed it into port.

The *Antelope,* laden with barley, got into the ice field before the crew realized the ship could not make port. The captain ordered the vessel hove to, and the anchors dropped. The ice closed in on the vessel. There the schooner remained for days, walled by ice, about a quarter of a mile abreast of the piers.

Wrecked at the Pier

At Milwaukee harbor
Lake Michigan
Sunday, April 14

Capt. James Gunderson put his boat, the tired schooner *Liberty,* to work early to make a few dollars carrying freight between ports on lower Lake Michigan. The Straits of Mackinac to the north were still chocked with ice, so most other vessels were still idled.

The schooner got caught in a snowstorm as it attempted to make Milwaukee harbor. The pilot was so blinded by the storm the *Liberty* got off course and struck a newly constructed pier where the government had not yet placed a light. The crash came with such force the timbers on the thirty-nine-year-old schooner crumbled, its bow was crushed, and the masts and rigging went by the boards. The schooner began to sink and the crew scrambled for the ratlines.

Help was nearby. Capt. William Kynaston, the man in charge of the harbor beacon, saw the accident. He ran out on the pier and threw a rope to the *Liberty,* then helped Gunderson and his small crew climb to safety. Gunderson's brother-in-law, Nicholas Thompson, didn't make it. He slipped as he was pulling himself from the deck, fell under the hull of the ship and was crushed to death.

The *Liberty* broke in two and its load of lumber ended up strewn along the beach. The cargo was salvaged. Some said the schooner was the oldest working wooden ship on the Great Lakes at the time.

*The **Messenger** got stranded in ice when the rudder broke off Manistee, Michigan. The crew went to shore in an open boat to get help. Courtesy Institute for Great Lakes Research.*

Fighting Death in a Small Boat

On Lake Michigan
Off Manistee, Michigan.
Sunday, April 14

Another early traveler on Lake Michigan was the propeller *Messenger*, carrying passengers and freight between Manistee, Michigan, and Milwaukee, Wisconsin. This boat got in trouble during the same storm that wrecked the *Liberty*. Shortly after leaving Manistee, after ramming its way through ice flows heaped along the shore and then steaming out into the teeth of that winter gale, the *Messenger's* rudder post collapsed. Without a rudder, the steamer drifted at the mercy of the storm. Because they were only a few miles out of port, four members of the crew volunteered to take a small boat to shore and get help. The trip became a battle of endurance against the elements. Afterwards, the sailors said they felt lucky to be alive. Before it reached shore, the boat got bound up in ice. The men struggled for hours against the ice flows, the gale and the wind until they finally reached the Manistee pier where they were taken aboard the schooner *William Jones*, moored there. The sailors got word ashore and a tug was sent. The *Messenger was* towed into Milwaukee.

A Gallant Rescue

On Lake Michigan
Off Grosse Point, Illinois
Monday, April 15

After watching the plight of the propeller *Messenger* the crew of the schooner *William Jones,* under the command of Capt. James Clark, got into some serious trouble of its own. The *Jones* set sail that same night from Manistee to Chicago with a cargo of lumber. The storm was still whipping the lake and it was a rough trip. The vessel developed a leak about midnight. The crew manned the ship's hand-operated bilge pumps until 11:00 AM Monday, when the *Jones* got close enough to shore to drop anchors. By then the sailors collapsed from exhaustion. Operating bilge pumps was hard work. Within an hour the ship waterlogged and the crew climbed into the rigging.

When the word reached Chicago that a schooner was in trouble about fifteen miles north of the city, the list of volunteers willing to help rescue the crew was almost overwhelming. Chicago was teeming with ships and sailors waiting for the 1872 shipping season to get underway. Capt. J. McGinn volunteered to go to the *Jones* with his tug the *Robert Tarrant.* He was joined by Capt. Orville W. Green from the bark *J. C. King,* Capt. William Gamble from the schooner *Harriet Ross,* Capt. Robert Lyons from the bark *Flying Mist,* Capt. Alex Quinn from the tug *McLane,* Capt. B. Brenier from the tug *Ben Drake,* Capt. John Jennings from still another unnamed vessel, and the regular crew of the *Tarrant,* engineer William Level, and sailors William Armstrong and Aleck McDonald. With ten rescuers packed aboard the tug, someone might have wondered if the vessel would have room for the seven sailors to be rescued from the *Jones.* Nevertheless, the *Tarrant* steamed boldly out of Chicago harbor about 3:30 PM that afternoon and put its bow into the heart of the gale that was still whipping Lake Michigan into a frenzy.

The *Tarrant* was alongside the *Jones* by 5:00 PM. The *Jones* was anchored but partly submerged about two miles offshore, and the crew was still clinging to the rigging to escape the seas washing over the deck. The seas were so high that nobody dared launch a lifeboat. Captain McGinn brought the tug under the lee of the stricken schooner and after several tries, made it fast so the crew of the *Jones* could come aboard. Rescued were Capt. Clark, mate George Mayo, steward L. Smith and sailors Robert Mitchell, Edward Anderson, Daniel Davis and a man known only as Bill. The *Tarrant* took everybody directly into Evanston, which was the nearest port. By then, the word was out that a rescue was in progress. When the tug steamed up to the dock, a crowd of people gathered to cheer.

The *Jones* did not capsize, but it took damage just the same. The seas washed the deck load of lumber away, and as the day progressed, the foresail, jibs and finally the jib boom also were carried away. The schooner was salvaged.

More Trouble With Ice

On Lake Huron
At Alpena, Michigan
Monday, April 22

When Capt. L. R. Boynton brought the propeller *Wenona* into Thunder Bay that afternoon, he discovered heavy ice still blocking Alpena's harbor. By 5:00 PM the ship worked its way to within a mile and one-half from shore, but could make no more progress. In some places, the ice was reported fifteen inches thick.

The ship remained there all night. In the morning, an ice plow was sent from Alpena to try to cut a channel, but it could not be done. That afternoon, five passengers, consisting of four men and one woman, walked across the ice to Alpena. Later, because of the novelty, hundreds of people from town walked out to visit the steamer. In the evening Boynton took the *Wenona* back to Detroit without unloading any of the cargo.

STEAMBOATS IN ICE

*Propeller **Wenona** was turned back by ice blocking Thunder Bay at Alpena, Michigan. Courtesy Institute for Great Lakes Research*

Wreck of the *Eva Cone*

On Lake Michigan
Port Washington, Wisconsin
Monday, April 22

    The schooner *Eva M. Cone* made a gallant show. With sails unfurled, the vessel boldly slipped through the drifting ice floes in Port Washington's harbor, heading for the open sea. The *Cone* was another one of the early vessels venturing out on Lake Michigan after a long and frigid winter. The little ship had sailed into Port Washington the day before from nearby Milwaukee, taken on a load of lumber, and was heading back to Milwaukee with it. Something unexpected happened. The vessel struck something just outside the harbor, damaged its rudder and punched a hole in the hull. The crew abandoned ship and came ashore in an open boat. The *Cone* flooded, rolled on its side, and the wreck later washed up on the beach.

15

Steamer ***Lawrence*** led a fleet of vessels that smashed their way through a massive ice blockade on Lake Ontario.

Steamboats In Ice

The propeller *Lawrence*, with Capt. A. Reed at the helm, steamed out of Ogdensburg, New York on Monday, April 22 with a full cargo, including eight paying passengers and nine horses, all bound for Oswego, New York. Reed knew that Lake Ontario was choked with a great field of ice, but the upper end of the St. Lawrence River was open and he gambled that the ice on the lake also was breaking up.

On arrival at Cape Vincent, near the head of the river, Reed found the steamers *Oswegatchie, Brooklyn, Young America, Empire* and *Milwaukee*, also loaded with cargo and waiting for the ice to melt or move. Prevailing westerly winds had the ice stacked in great blocks, piled on top of one another. The sailors were playing cards and smoking their pipes while shippers fumed and counted their losses. Reed sized up the ice, and decided to make a try. He ordered extra provisions and fuel put aboard at Cape Vincent, and by 2:00 PM Tuesday, the *Lawrence* was pushing out into Lake Ontario for the beginning of what turned out to be a week-long battle against shifting ice. When the *Lawrence* steamed out of port, the other captains decided to weigh anchor. They reasoned that if the *Lawrence* could cut a passage through the blockade, they would be smart to follow. As the word got around, other steamers joined the fleet. It wasn't long before the entire fleet was caught in a massive, shifting, unstable sea of ice that covered the northeastern part of Lake Ontario. Some of the passengers on the *Lawrence* later told the *Oswego Times* that it was the most unusual trip they ever took. They looked out over magnificent scenery. There was ice as far as the horizon and as many as thirteen steamers in view, all of them belching black coal smoke against the stark grey landscape as they rammed their way forward a few feet, then backed up to try again. The *Lawrence* sometimes found soft ice and made headway for a while, but then encountered blocks of ice from eight to ten feet thick, and spend hours ramming and pushing against it.

Days passed and still the battle went on. Progress sometimes was counted in terms of feet instead of miles. The passengers said they passed away their time with lively games of euchre. Everybody remained in good spirits throughout the ordeal. Even Captain Reed sat in on a few card games. He expressed confidence that the *Lawrence* would somehow find a way through the ice. His confident manner spread throughout the ship. Everybody seemed to enjoy their situation and nobody worried. There was plenty of food aboard for the passengers and crew but someone forgot to stock extra provisions for the horses. Within a few days the oats and hay were gone and the animals were starving. Their owner, Silas Randall, was among the passengers. He pleaded with Reed to help him find a way to get feed to his horses. Reed hailed some of the other steamers in the area and discovered that the *City of Boston* was loaded with corn. Randall and some of the crew members then went on a strange expedition across the ice. They dragged a lifeboat, sometimes using planks to help them get across patches of soft ice, and brought back enough corn to feed the horses for the rest of the trip.

The fleet remained locked in the ice from Tuesday afternoon until the following Sunday, April 28. By then the vessels had worked their way several miles south of the False Duck Islands. That morning, not long after sunrise, Reed discovered that a shift in the wind had opened a channel through the ice toward the north. The *Lawrence* was still in the lead, and when Reed turned the ship into the rift, the other captains faithfully followed. This led to still another patch of clear water that eventually brought the fleet out into clear water. The gamble paid off. All of the vessels made it through the ice.

Schooner Upside Down

On Lake Huron
Off Lexington, Michigan
Thursday, April 24

Imagine being trapped below decks to drown in a capsized schooner. It happened to a steward and deck hand on the *Jennie Graham* when an unexpected spring squall flipped the vessel upside down. The *Graham,* under the command of Capt. Duncan Graham, of Glencoe, Ontario, was without cargo, bound for Saginaw to pick up what may have been its first load of the season. The *Graham* was an empty schooner, under full sail, when at about 4:00 PM it got caught in one of Lake Huron's unexpected spring squalls packing high winds. Before the crew realized the danger and reefed sail, the ship capsized about eight miles offshore.

The two trapped crew members, identified only as a Norwegian and an Englishman, names unknown, were caught below deck. They died there, struggling in the dark, upside-down world of a flooding ship. The only escape for them would have been to do the unnatural thing. That was to dive into the rising water and work their way out through a series of doors and hallways to freedom on the deck, which was under them instead of above. Captain Graham also died. He was last seen clinging to two planks in the water and drifting away from the overturned ship. His body was recovered days later in the St. Clair River, south of Port Huron.

Seven members of the crew survived. They clung to the sides of the overturned wreck for about an hour until the ship unexpectedly turned back on one side. Once this happened, a life boat was exposed. The boat was cut away from the davits and the sailors scrambled aboard, happy at last to be out of the chilling waters of the lake. An hour later, their

*This drawing of the ill-fated **Jennie Graham** shows the vessel rigged as a barkentine. The **Graham** was described as a schooner when it capsized on Lake Huron. Courtesy Institute for Great Lakes Research*

luck got even better. The schooner *Sweepstakes* came along, picked up the shipwrecked crew, and took them to Lakeport, Michigan. One survivor had a broken leg.

The *Graham* was salvaged. It was towed into Port Huron and put in dry dock for repair. The top masts, all of the lighter spars, booms and gaffs, jib boom, sails and ropes were lost.

The Copper Strike

At the copper mines
Calumet, Michigan
Saturday, April 27

The strike began when a few miners at the Calumet and Hecla copper mines walked off their job for better pay and shorter hours. They said they wanted to work eight hours a day instead of ten, and wanted ten dollars a month pay instead of eight. As soon as the word got out, other miners thought the workers at Calumet and Hecla had a good idea so the strike spread. By Monday, April 29, the rest of the miners at Calumet and at nearby Schoolcraft were picketing. On May 3, miners at Copper Falls also were off the job. The copper mines at Quincy, Pewabic and Franklin were shut down by May 6. Before it was over, an estimated two thousand miners were picketing for better wages and shorter working days.

The situation seemed so threatening to Sheriff Bartholomew Shear of Houghton County, that Shear wrote to Michigan Governor H. P. Baldwin, asking for federal troops to help restore order. Baldwin sent a return telegram in which he said the nearest army troops, normally stationed at Chicago, were not available because they had been dispatched west to the plains. Shear decided on May 16 to take matters in his own hands. By then he had acquired the names of four strike leaders, and he sent a group of sixteen deputies . . . probably all of his regulars plus a few men brought over from adjoining counties . . . to arrest them. He hoped the arrests would help persuade the miners to quit hostilities and return to their jobs. Things didn't go well for the deputies. They found a group of about seven hundred strikers gathered at the gate when they arrived. When the arrests were made, the strikers rallied and surrounded the deputies, demanding that the men be let go. Several women, apparently wives of the strikers, also participated. The deputies were so outnumbered, and so intimidated, that they let the four men go and withdrew. Nobody was hurt.

The entire mood of the strike seemed to be one of jollity. As the days went on, the strikers shocked company officials with parades, singing and flag waving. Some of the workers who could play musical instruments organized a marching band for the occasion. When a small company of army troops and state police arrived at Portage, the strikers treated the whole thing as a big joke. They offered to send their marching band to Portage to escort the troops up to Calumet.

After a few weeks the strike began to show signs of losing strength. Many of the workers feared violence. At one meeting, a large number of the workers pressed to return to their jobs. They said they preferred getting wages to going hungry. At about that time, Mr. Agassiz, president of the Calumet and Hecla mine, made a trip from Detroit to the mine.

He apparently was a decisive man and a persuasive talker. Shortly after he arrived on May 22, the strike was broken. Agassiz ordered the miners back to work. If they failed to work, he said he would close down the mines and order everybody to move out of the company-owned houses. He offered slightly better wages, but said he would not agree to eight-hour work days. Eight strike leaders were quietly arrested.

That night the miners held a meeting to talk about Agassiz's offer. A majority of the workers voted to return to their jobs. When the meeting ended everybody marched through town to the company headquarters and "surrendered." It apparently was a gala affair because they brought the marching band.

Ramming Through The Straits

In the ice fields
At the Straits of Mackinac
Sunday, April 28

The propeller *Champlain*, under the command of Capt. R. McGrory made headlines when it became the first ship to get through the ice at the Straits of Mackinac. It took a few days to do it. The *Champlain* was steaming from Chicago to Ogdensburg, New York, with cargo, probably grain, and arrived at the straits on Wednesday, April 24. Captain McGrory first tried to pound a way through a channel of thin ice along the southern coast, but soon ran into blocks of ice up to eighteen inches thick. After spending the day ramming the ice, he backed his ship out of the field and dropped anchor in clear water for the night. The powerful wrecking tug *Prindiville* also was working in the area, trying to drive a route through the ice, but not having any luck either.

On Thursday morning, McGrory renewed his efforts, this time pushing the steamer into the ice along the northern edge of the straits. The blockade seemed at first to be just as heavy. Once he got started, however, McGrory found soft ice and had success working the ship for some depth into the field. From Thursday until Sunday night, the ship drove

STEAMBOATS IN ICE

*The **John Prindiville** was a well-known wrecking tug operating on the Great Lakes in 1872. Courtesy Institute for Great Lakes Research*

ahead, then backed up and pushed forward until it had forced its way through about one hundred miles of ice. After that, the open water of Lake Huron was in sight.

The word reached Chicago with electrifying speed. By the next day, an estimated one hundred vessels, most of them full of grain, steamed, sailed, or were towed out of Chicago, Milwaukee and several other ports. Most of them were grain loaded and bound for Buffalo. What they didn't know was that another massive ice blockade awaited them at Buffalo.

Collision at Marblehead

On Lake Erie
Off Sandusky, Ohio
Wednesday, May 8

The crew of the propeller *Granite State* later claimed that the scow *Forest Maid* had its lights mounted backwards, causing the night collision that sank the scow and left some of the crew members injured. The steamer's officers thought they were approaching the scow from behind. Instead of passing to starboard, the boats struck head-on at about 11:00 PM. The accident happened between Lake Erie's Kelleys Island and Marblehead, on the Ohio mainland. The *Granite State*, carrying both passengers and cargo, was steaming west on a course for Toledo. The scow was sailing east.

A passenger on the *Granite State* watched the collision. He said the steamer ran right over the little sailing vessel, taking very little damage to itself in the crash. The scow capsized and sank. Captain Stone and the five other members of his crew found themselves struggling together in the water. Everybody was rescued by the *Granite State* and put ashore at nearby Put-In-Bay.

Artist's drawing shows the **Granite State** *as it appeared at about the time it collided with the scow* **Forest Maid** *on Lake Erie. Courtesy Institute for Great Lakes Research*

STEAMBOATS IN ICE

The next day the tug *Mystic* found the smashed hull, still partly afloat off Marblehead, and towed it to a reef off Cedar Point where the wreck was stripped and given up for a total loss. A later story in the *Detroit Free Press* said a salvager towed the broken hull to Sandusky where it would be rebuilt.

The *Somerset* Wreck

On Lake Erie
Off Monroe, Michigan
Saturday, May 11

The tugboat *Zouave* arrived in Lake Erie Saturday night with six lumber laden barges in tow after a trip down the St. Clair and Detroit Rivers from Bay City, Michigan. At the end of the string of barges was the *Somerset*, laden with varieties of lumber and lathe for delivery at Monroe.

After reaching Monroe, the *Zouave* unhooked from the string, separated the *Somerset* from the pack much like a switch engine does cars on a railroad siding, and began turning the barge around for a short trip into the harbor. Something went wrong. The *Somerset* collided with the barge *Wolverine*, also in the string, took a hole in the side and sank. The crew was picked up by the tug.

The *Compound* Explosion

In Buffalo Harbor
Friday, May 10

The port of Buffalo, New York, was blocked by a super ice jam. The prevailing westerly winds pushed thousands of cakes of floating ice to the east end of Lake Erie where they formed a moving, shifting and almost impenetrable wall. The ice kept this important harbor closed long after shipping was underway on the rest of the lakes. Boats began arriving at the wall of ice, but found they could not get into Buffalo to unload cargo. Many captains dropped anchor and waited for someone to cut a channel through the obstacle. Other vessels tried to work their way into the harbor, either acting like ice breakers or searching for holes in the constantly shifting ice patterns. Inside the harbor, ships that spent the winter at Buffalo were loaded with cargo and waiting to get out. Frustration was high. Big business was at a standstill. Hundreds of thousands of dollars were being lost daily for want of a way through the blockade.

A battery of harbor tugs was busy hammering on the ice in hopes of breaking open a route. Among them were the heavy tugs *Compound*, under the command of Capt. John Wysoon, and the *Wadsworth*, with Capt. Ed Thorpe at the helm. The two tugs went out together on Friday morning, with schooners in tow, and were working side-by-side. The plan was to hit the ice blockade with a double strike of tugboat power. It had been a long and difficult morning. The *Compound* and *Wadsworth* spent the time ramming the ice, then backing up to slam into it again. It was grueling, bone-jarring work for the crews. Every time the boats hit the ice, they came to a sudden, crunching halt, and anybody who was not hanging on was in danger of being thrown to the deck. The boats were making some progress. They were about a mile from the inside lighthouse, far enough out in the lake that few people on shore were watching.

The residents of Buffalo were jolted by a concussion at 1:15 PM. It was loud enough that every head turned. People ran out in the streets to learn its source. Binoculars were turned toward the lake, and the word spread like wildfire through the town; the *Compound* had exploded! The first reports said that the vessel was "blown to atoms and sunk" and that all members of the crew were dead. Later, when the *Wadsworth* steamed up to the dock, it was carrying all members of the *Compound's* crew. Everybody was still alive although some of the sailors were seriously injured. Captain Thorpe said most of the men were on the deck where the force of the blast threw them into the water. The others managed to jump overboard before the tug turned partly on its starboard side and sank in shallow water. The cook, George Burridge, died the next day from the scalding he took in the face, chest and arms. The explosion caught Burridge in the ship's galley, washing dishes. Unlike the other men, who were dressed in heavy coats and nearly all at work somewhere on the open deck, Burridge was the most vulnerable. He was working in a hot, steamy part of the ship. Not only was he not wearing a protective coat, but his shirt sleeves were rolled up. When the blast came, he was cooked alive by the steam. Fireman Alex McLean risked his own life to enter the wrecked cabin and pull Burridge to the deck moments before the *Compound* capsized and sank. McLean was scalded in the face, but he recovered.

Captain Wysoon was pulled from the water with serious injuries to his head, hip and left hand. He recovered. Engineer Timothy Corbine was slightly scalded and bruised. The other two members of the *Compound's* crew, assistant fireman Thomas McNichols and deckhand Charles Starboard, were not hurt, but both men were badly frightened and suffering from cold when they were removed from the water.

There was speculation that the explosion was caused by ice chunks plugging the water intake pipe. Engineer Corbine disputed that theory at an inquest the next week. He said he had been in the engine room just minutes before the explosion, checked the water level, and was sure that the boiler was filled. He said the steam pressure was at eighty-five pounds, well within the approved ninety-five pound limit set by local boiler inspector William Moses. Moses, however, said he hadn't been around yet to examine the *Compound's* boilers. He said the operating permit issued in 1871 expired on the day of the explosion. He believed the boiler had a defect.

The *Compound* was raised the next month. It was said the damage was extensive. The boiler was found to have one side blown away. The force of the blast went aft, so most of the damage to the ship was in the stern. That probably saved most of the crew. They were either working amidships or in the bow, away from the force of the explosion. Nearly all of the wooden superstructure was shattered. Captain Wysoon was hurt because he was working in the pilothouse, which was demolished.

STEAMBOATS IN ICE

*This rare photo shows the steamer **Chicago** at Milwaukee in 1869. The ship was holed by ice and partially sunk trying to get into Buffalo in May, 1872. Courtesy Institute for Great Lakes Research.*

Saving the *Chicago*

In the Ice Fields
On Lake Erie
Monday, May 13

Two days after the *Compound* disaster, nothing was changed at Buffalo harbor. If anything, the wall of ice had gotten thicker. A fleet of ships stood at anchor about fifteen miles out in the lake, waiting for the blockade to either melt or the wind to blow it away. The tugs at Buffalo continued to hammer away from the inside until nearly every one of these vessels became disabled. Steamers on the outside also rammed the ice, trying to find a way through. A few managed to get in, while others found themselves stranded in the ice. Some reports said about ten steamers and nearly seventy sailing ships could be counted among the waiting vessels. Among them was the propeller *Chicago*, under the command of Capt. John Dissett, which had steam up and, like the others, was trying to bash a way into the port.

The *Chicago* ran into some bad luck. An ice slab cut a hole in the ship's wooden hull, and the vessel sank. It wasn't really a sinking. Nobody could explain why the ship waterlogged, and remained partially afloat. The weight of the engines alone usually pulled a steamship down. Some theorized that it was the wooden superstructure, which did not separate from the hull, that kept the *Chicago* from going to the bottom. Others thought the twenty-six thousand barrels of flour in the hold gave the ship its buoyancy. The tug *William A. Moore* pulled alongside the floating wreck and took off twenty-one crew members. Captain Dissett and a watchman, Peter Harris, elected to stay with the wreck to prevent salvage problems. Dissett declared that he would stay aboard while any portion of his command floated.

On Tuesday, the propeller *Ocean*, under the command of Capt. Walter Robinson, came upon the still floating wreck. Robinson suggested towing the *Chicago* into shallow water instead of letting it sink in the middle of Lake Erie. There was a problem with the plan. Fears were expressed that any pulling on the wreck might cause the superstructure to break free and the *Chicago* would sink. Dissett decided he was willing to take the risk and a tow line was made secure. The *Ocean* slowly put pressure on the hawser and the *Chicago* started to move out of the ice. Soon the two ships were in open water. The *Ocean* beached the *Chicago* on the south shore of Lake Erie, about a mile offshore and five miles west of Buffalo. The *Buffalo Morning Express* said in a story on May 15 that the ship was bow-in toward the shore, with the stern resting on the bottom of the lake in four fathoms of water and its forward cabins high and dry. Captain Dissett and watchman Harris now had drier and more secure quarters. Provisions were delivered, and the two men waited for the wrecking tugs.

Within hours tugs were at work on the *Chicago*. Lighters tied alongside the wreck and workers removed the ship's cargo of flour, one hundred barrels of wine, fifty barrels of Bethesda water, fifty barrels of ham and numerous other sundries that had been shipped from Chicago. Divers attached four large pontoons to the ship's hull, and they were pumped full of air. The wreck was afloat and safe at last. It was towed into Buffalo on May 17.

More Ice Casualties

On Lake Erie
In the great ice blockade

Other vessels got in trouble in Lake Erie ice during the month of May. Some of the things that happened:

▶ The schooner *Russell Dart* sank between the piers at Port Colborne, Ontario, on Saturday morning, May 4, when it struck a sharp piece of ice. The ship was loaded with wheat, bound from Toronto, Ontario, to Oswego, New York. The *Dart* was patched, the water pumped out, and it was towed to a local elevator where the grain was removed. Nearly five thousand bushels of wheat were damaged.

▶ The old lumber barge *Ocean* (not the propeller by that name) sank in nine feet of water off Point Albino after its wooden hull was stabbed by the ice. The Coast Wrecking Company couldn't salvage the wreck that summer. The barge was formerly the Ward Line steamer *Ocean*, once lauded as the finest passenger and freight hauler on the lakes.

▶ The schooner *William Young* tried to squeeze through a break in the ice at Buffalo on May 15, and got caught. The *Young* was loaded with coal bound for Chicago, and was in tow of a harbor tug when the ice squeezed in on the two vessels. The tug wasn't powerful enough to pull the *Young* through the ice, so the schooner was abandoned. As the ice shifted, the *Young* was driven up on Horseshoe Reef not far from the wrecked barge *Ocean*. The tug *Anderson* later raised the *Young* and towed it into Buffalo for repair. The ship was badly warped from its wintry ordeal.

▶ The tug *C. W. Jones* was cut open by the ice on Saturday, May 11. The pumps could not keep up with the leak so the ship was run ashore at Blackwell Canal.

New Era of Shipping

The launching of the new iron propeller *Cuba* at Buffalo on May 9 marked the beginning of a new era of aggressive commercial lake shipping. The Union Steamship Company built the *Cuba* and later its sister ships, *Java, Russia* and *Scotia,* with a vision for the future. They were all cast from the same basic mold. Measuring two hundred thirty-one feet in length, they were designed exclusively for freight, and they were among the first vessels on the lakes to contain water tight compartments for water ballast. The company wanted to be a tough competitor for the lucrative freight hauls between Chicago and Buffalo, and it did not want to waste time taking on bothersome low profit freight like sand, salt or coal for ballast on the return trips from Buffalo.

The *Cuba* offered some other innovative features that were ahead of its time. The steamer contained four water tight compartments, or bulkheads, that could be closed off in case the hull was damaged. It carried a new fluted lens signal lamp that could be seen for thirteen miles. The ship was powered by two, three hundred and fifty horsepower engines. The *Cuba* was a very successful ship. It remained active on the lakes for seventy-four years. It was operating under the name *Maplebranch* under Canadian ownership when scrapped in 1947.

Among the other super ships built in 1872 were:

▶ Railroad ferry *International,* launched at Fort Erie on July 17. This vessel measured two hundred twenty-six feet in length. It was built for the Grand Trunk Railroad and put in service at the St. Clair River between Port Huron, Michigan and Sarnia, Ontario.

▶ The propeller *Peerless* at Cleveland on June 8. The boat measured two hundred twenty-five feet.

▶ The schooner *Thomas W. Ferry* launched April 16 at Detroit was two hundred thirty feet long.

▶ *Camden*, a three masted schooner launched at Cleveland on April 20 was two hundred feet long.

▶ Schooner *Ahira Cobb* slid down the ways at Cleveland on May 13. It measured two hundred three feet in length.

STEAMBOATS IN ICE

The Cuba was one of the new breed of iron ships going on the lakes in the 1870s. Courtesy Institute for Great Lakes Research

▶ Canadian steamer *China* launched April 27 at Kingston, Ontario, boasted a capacity of fifteen thousand bushels of grain.

▶ The propeller *Menomonee*, launched September 7 at Menomonee, Michigan, was one hundred ninety-seven feet long.

For Safer Waters

U. S. Legislators were concerned about the large number of deaths aboard ships, not only on the Great Lakes but on the oceans of the world. Explosions, sinkings and fires were happening too frequently. Investigations revealed that in many cases, steamship companies might have prevented many deaths if they had used some common sense in designing, equipping and operating their vessels. Congress passed an important steamship law in the spring of 1872 that required passenger ships to carry enough lifeboats to handle all passengers carried. It was a law that never should have had to be written. One newspaper, in lauding the bill, noted that some steamboat companies were so anxious to make money, they thought nothing of risking a major disaster by overloading their ships.

The law had a few other bites. Ships between five hundred and fifteen hundred tons were required to carry a minimum of three fire extinguishers. All vessels were prohibited from using kerosene oil in their lamps, which seemed to be the source of many fires at sea. Whale oil and other safer sources of lighting were available. Thomas Edison was around and probably already thinking about ways to use electricity to make artificial light. The law also required ship's boilers to be made of iron and each plate stamped by the manufacturer with the number of pounds of tested strength allowed per square inch. Manufacturers were subject to fines of up to one thousand dollars for turning out defective boilers.

Safety aboard sailing ships also was addressed. Many tall ships were sunk in collisions with steamships during fog and in night travel. A new regulation changed standards for the use of fog horns and lamps. Sailing ships were required to do the following: When on a starboard tack, sound one blast of the horn. When on the port tack, sound two blasts. When with the wind free or running large, sound three blasts. When at anchor, sound general alarm. All signals were to be sounded at two minute intervals. When approaching a steamship at night, sailing vessels were required to show a lighted torch on the quarter most visible to the steamer. Vessels navigating rivers at night, without the tow of a steamer, would sound a fog horn every two minutes.

The *Marquette* Miracle

On Lake Huron
Off Presque Isle
Saturday, May 18

When the propeller *Annie Young* found the schooner *Marquette* in a sinking condition, things looked hopeless. The schooner, loaded with twenty-two thousand bushels of corn, had developed a leak in heavy weather. Some thought the ship hit something; perhaps a drifting log. It had three feet of water in the hold and the rush of water could clearly be heard gushing through an open wound in the hull. The crew was

*The schooner **Marquette** was miraculously saved from sinking in Lake Huron by a fish. Courtesy Institute for Great Lakes Research*

busy with the hand-operated bilge pumps, but it appeared to be a losing battle. The schooner was settling even as the crew of the *Young* watched.

The sailors on the *Young* did what they could to save the *Marquette* anyway. They attached a tow line and steamed off toward Cheboygan, Michigan, even though nobody expected to make port before the ship was lost. Strangely enough, when the *Young* finally steamed into port, the *Marquette* still was trailing faithfully along behind. Even stranger, the schooner wasn't riding any lower in the water than when it started the trip.

The *Marquette*'s crew said they could not explain the phenomenom. They said the noise of the water rushing into the hold stopped and the ship quit sinking shortly after it began its trip to Cheboygan. How could this have happened? An investigation revealed that a large fish got caught in the hole and plugged it. The fish saved the *Marquette*.

Strange Sinking of the *Fulton*

At Bay City dock
The Saginaw River
Sunday, May 19

The decks on the old schooner *Fulton* were stacked high with three hundred twenty thousand feet of lumber. The vessel was waiting to join one of the many endless chains of lumber barges tied behind steamers bound for eastern states, often via Tonawanda, New York. Before the *Fulton* left the dock this day, however, the vessel gave an unexpected lurch and sank. Crew members barely had enough warning to escape as the ship made its plunge to the bottom of the river.

Owners P. Stewart and L. L. Slifield of St. Clair, Michigan, hired a diver who found that the *Fulton* had a large hole in its stern. The hole was repaired, the ship pumped out, and soon everything was right again. Right except for the unexplained mystery. How did it happen? How does any ship take a hole in its stern, while moored quietly at a dock, and without anybody knowing about it? And how did it happen at the stern?

Another unanswered question: When did the *Fulton* get this hole? It was large enough that it sank the ship within minutes. Yet the *Fulton* had been moored at that place for more than a day. The vessel had been loaded several hours earlier and then was left standing quietly at the dock, waiting for a steam barge to take it in tow. Nobody could explain how the schooner collided with something in the river while it wasn't moving. If something struck the ship, the sailors on its decks should have noticed. They said it never happened.

Collision in the Fog

On Lake Michigan
Somewhere off Milwaukee, Wisconsin
Friday, May 24

Capt. James Finegan was on the alert. It was early in

the morning and as he stood on the quarterdeck of the schooner *Sam Robinson,* Finegan's senses were alert to the muffled sounds from an approaching steamer veiled by a heavy fog. The danger of collision was always present when ships moved in fog, and he wasn't anxious to have anything happen to the *Robinson.* Finegan shared part ownership of the ship that had been his home for several years. In addition to that, the captain was personally fond of the old boat.

The *Robinson* had its sails out, drawing from the faint winds, and was slicing north from Chicago at the slow pace of only four miles an hour. Finegan knew there wouldn't be much chance to turn his ship out of harm's way if the steamer got too close. He ordered the schooner's fog horn cranked frequently, letting the other vessel know that it was in the area.

Then, at about 7:30 AM, the lights of the propeller *Manistee* broke through the mist about one hundred feet off the starboard bow. Finegan's worst fears were coming true. The *Robinson* was on a collision course. He ordered the wheelsman to turn hard to port and called his crew to the deck to prepare for the crash. Even as the last man was scrambling up the ladder, the bow of the steamer hit the *Robinson* square amidships. The crash knocked men to their knees. The steamer seemed to keep coming, its massive bow cutting and stabbing the schooner with an unbearable crunching, snapping sound until the *Robinson* was sliced two-thirds of the way across the deck. Some of the cargo of corn that would never make its destination to Kingston, Ontario, spilled out in the lake as the two ships separated.

The *Robinson* sank so fast it capsized even as the *Manistee* backed away. The wreck went over on its starboard side, the masts smashing the *Manistee's* pilot house and cabins, damaging the steamer's superstructure, and carrying away the rail on the promenade deck. In the meantime, all eight members of the *Robinson's* crew were concentrating their efforts on getting the lifeboat launched. They got away moments before the *Robinson* went over. The sailors were picked up by the *Manistee* and taken to Milwaukee.

The *Robinson* lies in deep water, about forty miles east of Milwaukee. The ship was sixteen years old and measured three hundred sixty-nine tons.

Bad Night for the *Josephine*

At the mouth of the Saginaw River
Near Bay City, Michigan
Monday, May 27

The schooner *Josephine* was in trouble within minutes after it arrived on the Saginaw River from Saginaw Bay.

Event number one: The schooner collided with the tugboat *James T. Ransom,* which was steaming down the river with the barge *Detroit* in tow. The *Josephine's* jib boom poked the side of the *Ransom's* stack, causing it to disconnect and fall over. Then the schooner careened out of control and collided with the *Detroit.* The damage to the three ships was light. The captain of the *Josephine* probably suffered more because he had his pride badly singed. He moored the ship at one of the lower mill docks for the night and went to bed.

Event number two: That night the tug *William H. Pringle* with barges in tow steamed up the river. The *Pringle* got too close to the docks and the barge *Harvey Bissell* rammed the *Josephine* broadside, this time doing extensive damage.

The Wreckers

Saving wrecked, grounded, and sunken ships on the Great Lakes was big business in 1872. Shipwrecks were so common that newspapers almost gave new meaning to the word disaster. Every accident that happened to a vessel, from a harbor collision that caused a few thousand dollars in damage, to a fire at sea, was listed in the daily issue of the *Chicago Inter Ocean* under a headline proclaiming a menu of current disasters. There were so many vessels plying the lakes that accidents happened almost as frequently as automobile accidents occur today. Shipwrecks were not as easy to fix or clean up after as automobile accidents. Because of their great size and weight, it took people with special talents and super tools capable of handling vessels ranging from three hundred to two thousand tons. (The vessels of 1872 were midgets compared to the colossal sized ships plying the lakes today, and

*Capt. Frank Danger built a reputation as a colorful salvager of wrecked ships with the wrecking tug **Winslow**. Institute for Great Lakes Research.*

still getting into trouble.)

Tugboat captains who specialized in salvage operations developed reputations among the people in their trade, and sometimes, when a skipper came along with a name like Captain Frank Danger, master of the wrecking tug *Winslow*, they gained public attention. The newspapers loved Danger, probably because his name sparked a touch of romance to the daily grind of stories about grounded and wrecked ships. The *Detroit Free Press* printed the following story about the salvage of the grounded steamer *East Saginaw*, on Saginaw Bay, in April, 1875:

> *A telegraphic dispatch was sent to Capt. S. B. Grummond at this port for assistance, and in reply the powerful tug **Winslow**, Capt. Frank Danger, carrying two steam pumps, a diver and hawsers, left here yesterday afternoon for the scene of the wreck. Inasmuch as Captain Danger and his boat generally get what they go for, the **East Saginaw** will probably be at this port in a day or two for repairs. Last season, Captain Danger brought the steam barge **Fayette** to this port, the first wreck of the season, and*

> about the seventh of December arrived with the last wreck of the season, that of the schooner **Dolphin**. Evidently Danger is ahead, as the **East Saginaw** is the first wreck this season.

The tugboats engaged in salvage operations also tended to have colorful names that reflected great strength. Such boats as *Torrent, Vulcan, Hercules, Samson, Rescue, Magnet,* and *Leviathan* became part of the everyday fabric of Great Lakes shipwreck stories. The newspapers called them wrecking tugs or wrecking steamers, and they were just exactly that. They were larger than most harbor tugs and each of them especially designed for salvage work. The *Leviathan,* which was among the best known wreckers in its day, measured one hundred twenty-five feet in length. Each tug was equipped with heavy cables, or hawsers for pulling. They also carried steam powered pumps, canvas for quick-patching holes in ship's hulls, and when all else failed, they used pontoons large enough to raise ships from the bottom.

No salvage operation would be complete in 1872 without divers. These were daring men who daily put their lives on the line. Anyone who remembers actor John Wayne's staged drowning in the Hollywood film *Wake of the Red Witch* can grasp the conditions these divers worked in. They wore a canvas suit with heavy lead ballast boots. A large brass bell was fitted over their head that received air through a thin rubber hose from a pump from the deck of the vessel anchored above them. There was a small window in the brass bell through which the diver looked out. The diving suits were extremely bulky, sometimes leaky, and always dangerous. Yet these men were capable of working at depths of over one hundred feet of water, and they succeeded in raising sunken vessels long after they were written off as lost by their owners. F. Merriman and John Quinn, were among the well-known divers of the period.

Problems of salvage varied. No two wrecks were alike. Ships grounded on sand, in mud and on rocks, and sometimes in a combination of all three. Occasionally a boat came down on a large boulder that first put a hole in the bottom and then projected up through the hull, locking it in place and making it impossible for tugs to pull the vessel back into deep water.

*The wrecking steamer **Leviathan** was one of many vessels engaged in raising wrecked vessels in 1872. Courtesy Institute for Great Lakes Research.*

When ships sank, they often had large holes in their hulls from collision, foundered in a storm, or developed a leak from some weakness that developed in the hull. To raise a sunken ship, wreckers had to find the hole and plug it before pumping air back into the hull. When that failed, pontoons were attached to the hull and then filled with air.

When they went aground, the wrecking crew had to find some way of making the vessel lighter so that it could be floated back into deep water. If filled with cargo, lightening a grounded vessel sometimes only involved the removal of enough of the cargo to increase the buoyancy. If no cargo existed, salvagers resorted to other tactics such as removing fuel and any other things that might help lighten the ship, pulling with hawsers attached to several tugs, and, if all else failed, digging away the ground that held the vessel captive. Some salvage operations took weeks and even months to complete. Not all were successful.

Some case histories from 1872:

The wrecking steamer *Magnet* brought the brig *Henry Rooney* into port in May after a long struggle to get the vessel off a Lake Erie beach near Fairport, Ohio. The *Rooney* went ashore with a load of heavy square timbers in the hold the previous fall. During the winter, the hold also filled with sand. Before anything could be done to pull the brig off the beach, workers spent days at heavy labor, removing the timbers and shoveling away the sand. When the hull was finally empty, the *Rooney* still remained stuck fast on the sandy beach. The tug *S. S. Coe* brought a dredge, which dug a trench up to and around the ship. Once afloat, it was found that the *Rooney's* hull was still in excellent condition. The vessel turned out to be a valuable prize.

The heavy iron ship *Merchant* proved to be a special problem when it struck a rock and sank in shallow water at the mouth of the Detroit River on May 20. The steamer, under the command of Captain Briggs, was on its way from Buffalo to Chicago with railroad iron and general merchandise. The *Merchant* sank to the main deck. As it settled to the

*The iron-hulled propeller **Merchant** created a challenge for salvagers when it struck a rock and sank on the Detroit River. Institute for Great Lakes Research.*

uneven floor of the river, the vessel listed so severely to port that the sailors feared it would capsize. The wrecking tugs *Magnet* and *Hercules* were the first to arrive. They brought lighters to take off the cargo, four steam powered pumps and pontoons. The *Merchant* was a very heavy ship. It had a wooden hull covered with iron plating, much like the famed Civil War gunboat *Merrimac*. The *Detroit Daily Post* on May 24 said five steam pumps were working from the main deck, and two pontoons were attached, but they were not enough to refloat the ship. Reinforcements arrived. By May 26 the steamers *Mackinaw* and *Sweepstakes* were on the scene and two more pontoons were attached. By May 28 newspapers said a total of six pontoons were surrounding the stricken ship. This was enough. The *Merchant* was a most unusual sight, surrounded by pontoons and with five noisy steam pumps spewing heavy streams of water over the sides. The tugs *Sweepstakes* and *Magnet* shared in the tow up the river to Detroit's dry dock. Workers later said the ship had two holes in its side; one of them a gash twenty-three feet long.

The salvage of the propeller *Evergreen City* from Lake Erie's Long Point was another spectacular project. The ship, laden with general merchandise and passengers, was stranded in a November storm the year before. When Captain Riley took the job with his tug *Hercules,* it was obvious he had a lot of work to do. The shifting sand by then had surrounded and filled the hull. Vandals removed most of the cargo, stripped the ship of its windows, tools, dishes, crockery, and even carried away the marble tops to the wash stands. Riley brought a dredge, a steam pump and a lot of personal determination with him. By early July he had the *Evergreen City* refloated. He towed the wreck to Buffalo, where it was rebuilt as a steam barge.

The profits from a successful salvage operation were high, so the competition for salvage work was strong. Many tug owners were willing to pick up a salvage job in addition to their normal line of work, which was helping ships in and out of port, and towing them up and down the various rivers that link the Great Lakes. A captain's protest of a bill for refloating the schooner *Wanderer,* after it went aground on the Detroit River, reveals the kind of money wrecking crews were asking for their services. In his complaint, Captain James

Whitworth said his bill was seventeen hundred dollars, which was almost half the estimated value of his ship. He said he had just purchased the *Wanderer* for a down payment of a thousand dollars, and still owned another three thousand dollars. After it went aground, Whitworth hired the tugs *F. A. Bartlett* and *Favorite* to pull his ship free again. The tugs worked for ten dollars an hour, each, and the job took three days. In addition, a lighter was brought in for an additional ten dollars an hour, shovelers were paid to move the cargo to the lighter, a heavy towing cable was broken, and Whitworth was charged for having his vessel towed to dry dock, plus dry dock fees.

The *Favorite's* bill was four hundred and forty-five dollars. The *Bartlett* charged two hundred and fifteen dollars. The lighter, which remained on the job for eighty-six hours, got eight hundred and sixty dollars. The shovelers were paid eighty dollars. The broken cable cost Whitworth another eighty dollars. The towing vessel got ten dollars and the dock fee was another ten dollars.

Wrecking tug **Favorite** *was operating on the Detroit River in 1872. Courtesy Institute for Great Lakes Research.*

Summertime Troubles

June 1 - August 31

Fire on the *Dove*

At Amherstburg, Ontario
On the Detroit River
Thursday, June 4

The steamer *Dove* was nearly destroyed by fire from an overheated boiler while docked at the Canadian port of Amherstburg.

It was evening and the dock workers were busy exchanging cargo and preparing the ship to take on passengers when fire was discovered in the wooden deck just above the boiler. An alarm was sounded and the crew responded quickly. Fire hoses were strung and the lines charged. The local fire department also was called.

For a while it looked as if the fire would destroy the *Dove*. The fire fighters fought hard, and within the hour the blaze was under control. The *Dove* was saved, but not before its cabins took extensive damage.

Saving the *Giant*

On Lake Erie
Off Port Stanley, Ontario
Tuesday, June 4

The bark *American Giant* got in rough seas and started taking on water. The ship was loaded with wooden barrel staves made at Bay City, Michigan, and sailing across Lake Erie for O. S. Storrs Co., of Buffalo, New York when the storm struck. As the power of the storm gained, the ship became waterlogged and unmanageable. Heavy seas carried away a deck load of twenty-five thousand staves. The cabin was flooded. Crew members considered either abandoning ship or climbing into the rigging and praying for help. For all practical purposes, the *American Giant* was sunk. Wooden ships loaded with wooden cargos sometimes didn't completely sink.

They just get partly submerged. The condition was called waterlogged. This crew got lucky. Before things got too serious, the steamer *Mendota* came out of the gloom and took the vessel in tow to Buffalo. The two vessels arrived on Wednesday afternoon.

Boat masters reported passing through a sea of barrel staves in the middle of Lake Erie for days after that.

Hogged Out

At Point Albino
On Lake Erie
Sometime in early June

There was a phrase among mariners during the days of wooden ships that described warped decks and hulls. They said the vessel was "hogged out." It was a terrible thing to see a ship get in this condition because it meant that the original grace and beauty built in the vessel by its designer was gone If saved, it would take much skill to put the hull back in its original form again.

The bark *Colonel Ellsworth* got "hogged out" after it went ashore on Point Albino, Ontario. The hull split when the *Ellsworth* hit the rocks and eight thousand bushels of corn in the hold got wet. Before wreckers arrived with lighters to take off the cargo and pull the bark free, the corn absorbed the water, the cargo expanded, and put pressure on the ship's hull and deck from the inside. Sailors who visited the wreck said the deck developed a large hump amidships and the hull was warped outward from the pressure.

The *Ellsworth* was towed to Buffalo on June 14 for rebuilding.

*The tug **Balize** was towing lumber rafts from Michigan to Tonawanda, New York, in 1872. Courtesy Institute for Great Lakes Research.*

The *Ransom* Affair

On the Niagara River
Near Tonawanda, New York
Saturday, June 8

By early June the lumber barges and rafts from the Midwest were steaming into Tonawanda, where mills prepared the wood for shipping east to New York. It was in the afternoon and the tug *Balize*, with Capt. John P. Young at the helm, arrived with a string of lumber rafts from Michigan. The tug *James T. Ransom,* commanded by Capt. Asa Ransom Jr., was on the river to help the *Balize* jockey the

47

cumbersome rafts into place. The *Ransom* got a cable tangled in its wheel which caused the tug to capsize. Captain Ransom, four other members of the crew, and a passenger, Charles Smith, owner of the lumber raft, all found themselves unexpectedly swimming for their lives. Ransom and Smith were killed. They were last seen swimming from the overturned tug toward the nearest raft, but they didn't made it. Both men either were overcome by the cold water, or they got drawn under by the river currents and drowned. The *Balize* pulled the others from the water alive.

Remembering the *Maine*

At Goose Bay
On the St. Lawrence River
Sunday, June 9

  The hard luck ship *Maine* sank at Goose Bay, a spot along the St. Lawrence River below Alexandria Bay. The accident happened while the steamer was stopped to take on wood. About eight cords were loaded before someone noticed that the ship was sinking. The captain called for steam and then backed the *Maine* into the bay where it came to rest on a sandy bottom. The ship remained there, sunk, until the tug *Crusader* arrived from Detroit about a week later, patched a hole in the hull, and then used two steam pumps to remove the water. The *Maine* was towed to Ogdensburg for repair.
  Nobody knew for sure just why the *Maine* sprang that leak. Workers said the hull appeared to have been pierced by a rock. The captain speculated that it might have happened while the ship was passing through the Welland Canal on its last trip down.
  During its long career, the *Maine* was a jinxed ship. It exploded its boiler off Ogdensburg on July 5, 1871, killing five people and wounding two others. The 1872 sinking was the second of a long series of accidents. Fire was its final enemy. The *Maine* burned in May, 1880 at Port Huron, Michigan, burned a second time in April, 1898, at Tonawanda, New York, then was destroyed by a final fire on the St. Clair River near Marine City, Michigan, in July, 1911.

Dragging Bottom

The drought conditions that contributed to the forest fires across Michigan and adjoining states in 1871, also brought a serious drop in lake levels. The problem became especially critical by the spring of 1872. Key connecting channels between the lakes, like the notorious St. Clair Flats at the bottom of the St. Clair River, and even the water depths at the Welland and Saint Marys canals, were so seriously low that vessels couldn't pass with a full load. Loading and unloading ships at many ports had to be done with the help of lighters, or flat-bottom boats that carried cargo between shore and the ships anchored in deep water.

Help was on the way, at least at the St. Clair Flats, one of the worst of the trouble spots. In March Congress appropriated eighty-four thousand dollars for deepening and widening the channel. Plans were to deepen the main route to sixteen feet, which would be adequate to handle the largest vessels then on the lakes. It would be at least another year, however, before the work was done. In the meantime, the problem was as bad as it ever was going to get.

Some of the stories:

▶ The lumber barge *Eldorado* grounded at Ludington, Michigan, when trying to clear the harbor on April 14. About forty thousand feet of lumber had to be carried away on lighters before the barge was pulled free. The water depth measured about seven feet at a sand bar just off shore.

▶ On April 17, the propeller *Lake Breeze* found the water too shallow to reach the dock at Rock Falls, Michigan, with a load of merchandise, and returned the cargo to Port Huron. Communities along the shore were faced with the prospect of having to extend their docks farther out into the lake.

▶ Vessels at Chicago also were dealing with the low water. Ships discovered in April that they couldn't get out of the harbor if their draft exceeded twelve feet, six inches. A story in the *Chicago Inter Ocean* on April 27 said it took eight tugs a full day to drag the grain-laden eight hundred and thirty-two-ton bark *Erastus Corning* into the lake and get it on its way. The *Corning's* cargo had to be partly removed again at St. Clair Flats before it could clear that obstacle.

▶ That same day, the barge *Banner,* heavily loaded with lumber, hit bottom in Swan Creek at Toledo. It took two tugs to pull it back into deeper water.

▶ The first vessels attempting to clear the St. Clair Flats about May 1 discovered the water only eleven feet deep. Most boats of that period, when loaded, demanded thirteen feet of water to get clear. By May 6, about fifty ships were anchored at the head of the St. Clair River in Lake Huron, and another twenty-five vessels were waiting on the lower end while tugs and lighters worked to free the grounded schooners *D. P. Rhodes* and *George H. Ely* and the steam barge *Alleghaney.* The only way for many vessels to get through was to have lighters take off portions of their load and then reload after clearing the channel.

▶ The *Muskegon Weekly Chronicle* on May 1 reported massive log jams on the Muskegon River and its tributaries. "The water in the small streams is as low as it generally is in midsummer. The swamps have less water in them than they were ever before known to have."

▶ The *Detroit Free Press* reported on May 5 that the harbor at Collingwood, Ontario, was so shallow that much of the harbor was dried up. "Also ... Frenchman's Bay is crossed by people dry shod, an event unheralded since 1850."

▶ The propeller *Alaska* couldn't get to the dock at Manitowoc, Wisconsin, on May 6 because the water was too shallow. The ship had a draft of only eleven feet. Reports were getting out that the harbors at Sheboygan, Wisconsin, and Pentwater, Michigan, were also closed to shipping.

▶ The brig *Powhattan* grounded that same day while under tow on the St. Clair River near Port Huron. Two other barges in the tow, the schooners *Czar* and *Evaline,* couldn't stop and they collided one on top of the other. All three vessels were damaged.

▶ When the steam barge *W. T. Graves* arrived in Buffalo on May 24 with the schooners *George D. Russell* and *Annie Sherwood* in tow, Capt. Samuel Wood complained that it was "the most tedious and dragging trip" he ever experienced. He said the boats were delayed one day at the St. Clair Flats going up (on route to Chicago) and two days coming down. Wood said the boats were loaded about ten to fifteen percent lighter than normal, but they still had trouble.

The propeller **Vanderbilt** *was one of many vessels stuck in the mud in the St. Clair Flats during the 1872 shipping season. Institute for Great Lakes Research*

▶ The new iron propeller *Cuba* hit bottom at the St. Clair Flats on its maiden voyage from Chicago on June 12. The tug *Stranger* was assisting.

▶ The propeller *J. L. Hurd* went aground on Lake St. Clair on June 22. Two tugs, the *Urania* and *Wilcox,* worked with dredges for six days before the *Hurd* was pulled free again. The problem seemed so bad, the *Port Huron Daily Times* suggested jokingly that derricks be used.

▶ The *Toronto Daily Globe* reported on August 2 that the Welland Canal "is practically closed due to low water." The story said grain shippers in Buffalo were concerned because all available space for storing grain and other commodities there were filled due to the blockade.

▶ In September, Capt. M. Rathbun was named superintendent of a new government piloting and lighting service created at the St. Clair Flats to help vessels make passage. A pilot would be available to steer the ships through the channels, and if they were too heavy, a lighter was anchored there for immediate service.

▶ Complex problems developed at the flats as vessels waited for a chance to get clear of this frustrating obstacle. On October 14, the propeller *Forest City* was pulling the ore laden barge *William McGregor* through the channel and the *McGregor* grounded. The *Forest City* left the barge there and steamed on down the river to Detroit to get a hawser large enough to take the strain of pulling the *McGregor* through. In the meantime, another steamer entered the flats with the barges *James Couch, D. P. Dobbins* and a third unnamed vessel in tow. The *Couch* hit bottom and stopped, the *Dobbins* collided with the *Couch*, and the third barge hit the *Dobbins*. Tugs were called to help clean up the mess.

▶ Another serious jam happened in late November when the steamers *Vanderbilt, John Gould* and *Thomas A. Scott* grounded in the St. Clair Flats. The *Vanderbilt* was so hard on, it took wreckers several days to pull it free. Before the ship could be freed, a cargo of flour had to be removed to the steam barge *Mariner*. In the meantime, winter was setting in fast. Shippers were worried about being caught in the ice. Workers were frustrated by the delays. No sooner was the *Vanderbilt* freed on the afternoon of November 21, then the upbound schooner *Fred A. Morse* grounded at the same spot. The impatient captains of two downbound propellers decided to try to squeeze past and "wedged in alongside" the *Morse*. By the next day about thirty ships were anchored on the river, waiting to clear the flats before winter set in.

Union Trouble

On Lake Superior
Near Marquette, Michigan
Sunday, June 9

The propeller *Union* with the schooner *Cascade* in tow got caught in a blanket of fog. The crews lost their bearings and at 2:00 AM the boats both crunched to a jarring stop on Lake Superior's Laughing Whitefish Reef, twenty-four miles below Marquette, Michigan. They said the *Union* struck so hard the ship's bow lifted right out of the water.

It was starting out to be a bad season for the fifteen-year-old *Union*. The ship was aground the week before on Strawberry Reef in Green Bay. The boat's heavy iron hull helped it survive the two groundings without serious damage. The *Union* and its consort were hauling iron ore from

STEAMBOATS IN ICE

*The steamer **Union** had bad luck in 1872, Courtesy Institute for Great Lakes Research.*

Marquette to Green Bay.

The Burning *Kingston*

On the St. Lawrence River
At Grenadier Island, Ontario
Tuesday, June 11

In the seventy-three years that the steamer *Kingston* remained in service on the Great Lakes, from 1855 to 1928, its worst enemy seemed to be fire. Flames ravaged the ship twice in quick succession, in 1872 and again in 1873. The *Kingston* was partially burned again in 1905. Each time it was rebuilt to run again.

Flames did their first work on the *Kingston* on a fine summer afternoon in June, 1872, as the liner steamed up the St. Lawrence River from Brockville, bound for Toronto with about a hundred passengers and a full cargo of freight. When only twelve miles above Brockville the fire was discovered in a stateroom about amidships, directly over the engine room. The flames raced through the wooden superstructure with such speed that Captain Carmichael recklessly drove the

STEAMBOATS IN ICE

Kingston aground on Grenadier Island so the passengers would have a chance to escape. Only one lifeboat was launched. It was filled with women and children. The steamer was still moving and the boat swamped the moment it touched the water. Everybody else jumped overboard and worked their way ashore with the help of floating flotsam and life preservers. All but one of the people on that vessel escaped. A passenger, identified as Mrs. Jones of Montreal, drowned. It was said that she grabbed a life preserver, put it on, and then jumped from the stern of the burning ship. Her life preserver wasn't properly fastened and she didn't make it to shore. Some reports said a deck hand also drowned, but the story was never confirmed. The propeller *Dominion* later saw the burning hull and stopped to pick up the passengers and crew. They returned to Brockville on the *Dominion* that night.

The *Kingston* was completely rebuilt that fall and reappeared on the lakes as the *Bavarian* in 1873. About twenty people died when the *Bavarian* burned off Oshawa, Ontario, in Lake Ontario, that fall. The ship was named the *Algerian* when it burned the third time in 1905.

Dynamite was this vessel's last enemy. After serving the final years as the *John Donnelly,* a stripped down wrecking tug owned and operated by a Kingston, Ontario salvage

Fires plagued the steamer **Kingston.** *The first of three blazes ravaged the ship on the St. Lawrence River in 1872. One person died. Institute for Great Lakes Research.*

company, the hull finally had outlived its usefulness and was declared unseaworthy. The *Donnelly* was towed out on Lake Ontario where it was dynamited and sunk.

Strange Tides

Newspapers described the same phenomenon on Lakes Michigan and Ontario, at extreme opposite ends of the chain of lakes, on Thursday, June 13. Water levels dramatically rose and fell several feet within a few hours for no known reason. The *Milwaukee News* said the strange tidal action began about midnight when the water got so high it encroached the beach about twenty feet farther than anyone could remember. All that day the lake level fell to extreme lows and then returned, but it never got as high as it did in the first surge. Observers said the surface of the lake remained unusually flat while this strange phenomenon was going on. Even the normal swells stopped.

While people were standing in awe at the odd tidal events on Lake Michigan, the same thing was happening on Lake Ontario, according to the *Oswego Times*. At Oswego, New York, they said the water rose with great rapidity for fifteen to twenty minute periods, remained at that level briefly, then fell just as quickly. This happened five or six times between 3:00 PM and 5:00 PM. After this, the water remained at its lowest ebb until a gale developed late in the day. Once the storm hit, the lake returned to its normal level.

An unidentified fisherman who observed the phenomenon told about it in the *Rochester Democrat,* printed in Rochester, New York. He said he saw several men fishing in a small boat on Lake Ontario. When the tide went out, the boat was suddenly left in the mud, where there formerly had been about two feet of water. "They were surrounded by mud and sand. They left the stranded boat and while walking along the pier, the water returned. They got ready to go out in the lake once again, only to have the same thing happen about twenty minutes later." The same thing happen again and again all afternoon until a squall developed about 5:30 PM and the story teller left the lake. He said that when the water rose, it got about six inches higher than normal.

Aboard the *Sweepstakes*

On Lake Huron
Somewhere on Saginaw Bay
Friday, June 14

The lumber barge *Sweepstakes* sprang a leak and waterlogged in heavy weather off the Charity Islands. Things were looking rough for the crew. To save their ship and themselves, the sailors worked frantically jettisoning about fifteen thousand feet of lumber from the deck.

After a while, the propeller *Jenness* came upon the drifting *Sweepstakes* and took the vessel in tow for Port Huron. Once it arrived on the St. Clair River, the ship was found to be leaking so badly, a steam pump was put aboard for the next stage of the trip to Detroit dry dock. The barge was saved.

Launching the *Montana*

On the Black River
Port Huron, Michigan
Saturday, June 15

Port Huron shipbuilder Alexander Muir was embarrassed by the whole thing. The launching of his new two hundred thirty-six-foot long propeller *Montana* took three days to complete and may have been one of the longest, most drawn-out, and expensive affairs of its kind in Great Lakes history.

The launching was planned for Saturday. As was the custom in 1872, ships were built along the bank of a river and then skidded sideways into the water. A side launch was always a spectacular thing to watch and a crowd of people from the area gathered to watch. Workers pulled the stops out from under the skids and the *Montana* started rumbling down the ways leading down the river bank. A few brave men were standing on the deck of the ship, getting a firm grip on the railings for what was to have been a wild ride. Something unexpected happened. The unusually low water level caused by the drought, and a heavy bank of mud built up along the

STEAMBOATS IN ICE

*The **Montana** got stuck in the mud on the Black River when it was launched at Port Huron, Michigan. Institute for Great Lakes Research*

river brought the ship to a stop. There it remained stuck for the next three days. Muir hired a salvage company. The tugs *Brockway, Vulcan* and *General Burnside* attached hawsers and pulled on the fifteen hundred-ton hull, but it wouldn't budge. Dredges dug through the mud. Pontoons were attached. The tugs pulled and yanked some more. Hawsers snapped from the strain, but the *Montana* stayed stuck.

Port Huron newspapers made sport of the event. The ship in the mud became the joke of the town. The *Port Huron Times* editor wrote on Monday that since the unsuccessful launch, "people have been making the shipyard a place of resort."

A wrecking tug, the *Prindiville,* was brought to town. This vessel was an especially powerful vessel, built for ship salvage work. Once it put a line to the *Montana* and joined the three smaller tugs, the hull started to move. The *Montana* was finally afloat at 5:30 PM Tuesday, about seventy-five hours after the launch was started. The *Montana* proved to be a lucky ship after that. It enjoyed a forty-two year term of service, first as a passenger and freight hauler, and finally as a bulk freighter. It was destroyed by fire near Alpena in 1914.

The Waterspout

In Lake Huron
Off Rock Falls, Michigan
Thursday, June 20

People who live along the shores of the Great Lakes are familiar with waterspouts. They are strange windstorms at sea that resemble tornados. Instead of carrying dirt up in a long cylinder of whirling wind, they pick up tall, thin columns of water or vapor that sometimes rise hundreds of feet into the sky, then twist and shift like devil dancers until falling back into the sea. Sometimes several waterspouts are observed in the same area at the same time. Unlike tornados, waterspouts don't seem to be attached to thunderstorms. They usually extend down from a cumulus cloud into the lake. Waterspouts often happen late in the day, sometimes during what appears to be fair weather.

Waterspouts have occasionally been known to strike ships at sea. One such incident is believed to have happened near Rock Falls, Michigan, on the evening of June 20, 1872. The sailors aboard the schooner *Jamaica* first said it was a squall that capsized and sank their ship. Later they described the storm as a whirlwind that struck without warning. Two other nearby vessels were damaged by the same storm.

Capt. David Bothwell said the *Jamaica* was laden with eighteen thousand bushels of wheat bound from Milwaukee, Wisconsin, to Oswego, New York. He said the weather was fine and the winds were light and variable right up to the moment it happened. The crew finished the evening meal and everybody except Elizabeth Headington, the fifty-four-year-old cook, was on the deck. Bothwell said the wind seemed to strike from aloft, capsizing the ship in a single violent moment. All eight surviving members of the *Jamaica's* crew found themselves clinging to the side of the overturned ship. The men spent several anxious moments calling to one another, taking stock of what had happened and making sure everybody was still alive. Headington was the only one not accounted for. She was last seen in the cabin below, tending to her duties in the galley.

A few hundred feet away the schooner *Lucinda Van Valkenburg* lay becalmed, with its masts standing like bare sticks over the decks. The storm stripped the vessel of its sails and rigging. The schooner *Timothy Baker*, also in the area, lost its jib sail and jib boom. The wind carried away one of the ship's anchors and chain. The sailors described the storm as a tornado.

The incident was observed by the crew of the schooner *Starlight*, which was moored nearby at White Rock. They sent a yawl to the *Jamaica* and took everybody ashore before the schooner sank in fifty-three feet of water. As the *Jamaica* went down, it turned upright so that it settled gently on the bottom, with the top of the sails and masts showing above water. It was not hard for Capt. G. W. Chadwick, master of the Coast Wrecking Company's tug *Rescue*, to find the *Jamaica* a few days later. A diver was sent down, and pontoons were attached. The wreck was raised on the Fourth of July. It was towed to Port Huron for repair.

The damage was extensive because by the time the *Jamaica* was raised, the grain in the holds had swollen, causing the seams to open, some beams to crack, and the decks to raise. Chadwick said the diver found Elizabeth Headington standing upright in the galley where she died, her arms extended, her fists clinched, and her face locked in a grimace of terror. It was an image he took to his grave.

Power Boats on the Erie Canal

The quest by big business for bigger profits brought about constant change on the Great Lakes, including the vessels that traveled on the Erie Canal. While the canal was a success, the people who shipped goods from Buffalo to Albany, New York, and back again, were getting anxious for better service. The barges moving on the canal were too small, and the horses that pulled them too slow. The demand was for more goods shipped faster, to accommodate the increased volume of cargo delivered by larger and faster steamboats plying between Chicago and Buffalo. Steam powered barges were tried, but they didn't work out at first. Both paddle-wheeled vessels and barges with propellers caused a wash that wore down the canal's earthen embankments. Another serious problem: the cost of the coal needed to fuel the barges on the long trip across the State of New York was so high, barge men claimed they made more money letting the animals do the work, even though the trip took longer. It was clear that something else was needed, but what? It was a dilemma. Some old-fashioned American ingenuity was needed.

In 1871, the New York legislature appropriated a prize of one hundred thousand dollars to be awarded to the inventor who produced the first successful patent for a vessel that could replace the animal-driven barges. By 1872 the race was on. One dream-scheme followed another as inventors sent their ideas first from all over the United States and eventually the world. Before the year was over, some of the experimental vessels were being tested on the canal.

Many of the ideas were creative. Others were extremely complex and difficult to understand. Still others were totally ridiculous. Inventors wanted to propel boats by air propellers mounted on the stern, power operated poles attached to the sides, or pole-like feet marching along the bottom of the canal and attached to a turning wheel located in the center of the vessel. Submerged railroad tracks and cables were a popular thought. Some inventors wanted to draw the barges with elevated cables, others thought of submerged cables, and still others wanted to attach the cables to the canal bank.

The "syphonic system" was among the strangest ideas. A story in the April 16 edition of the *Toledo Blade* described it as follows: "the power to be derived from water supplied by a trough to be elevated above the canal and to extend its entire length, which is passed through a siphon, the short leg of which is to be inserted in the trough, and the long leg to pass through the stern of the boat. A flywheel placed over the stern of the boat and designed to receive and store up power, to be exerted by the crew during their leisure from other duties, and to deliver it again through the medium of a screw propeller connected with it by proper gears."

A man named Henry Stanley developed a way to propel a string of boats powered by two steam engines on the first and last barge in the chain. His idea was to power the lead boat with two screws off the bow, each projecting water back along the sides and under the hull. The last boat in the chain had two screws working at the stern, designed to draw the churning water from the sides of the boats and discharge it directly aft. Stanley visualized each boat in the middle being unencumbered by steam engines and fuel, so they would be capable of carrying up to two hundred and forty tons of freight, each. Four such barges would carry a total payload of nearly one thousand tons.

C. H. Jenner of Brockport, New York, proposed to mount a propeller in a chamber at the bow of the boat. The propeller pushed the water out through two long tubes passing through the ship and sending it out at the stern like dual rockets. Jenner said in his application for a patent that he believed the vessel could also be steered by the opening and closing of valves over the jets of water, thus eliminating the need for a rudder.

A canal boat built by Charles Hengery caught the attention of newspapers in September. It was another version of Jenner's idea. A section in the stern was cut away, and the propeller wheel was mounted there inside a three-foot long tube that could be turned and thus used as a way to steer the

Canal barges are tied around a moored schooner at the Erie Canal Basin and elevator at Buffalo. Loudon Wilson collection, Institute for Great Lakes Research.

ship. This vessel was actually built and tried on the canal.

Before it was over, it was clear that the winning vessel was going to be a propeller-driven steamboat with a propeller designed to avoid severe prop-wash. The first boat of this type appeared on the canal in late June. It was the *William Newman,* a one hundred-ton barge that boasted a propeller that forced the water directly astern as the vessel moved forward. The vessel could travel through the canal at an average speed of three miles-per-hour, which was faster than a horse or mule could pull it. On its first trip, owner Jerry Small said the vessel used twenty-five tons of coal, at a cost of one hundred thirty-seven dollars and fifty cents. An engineer was paid thirty dollars in wages. Small said that by comparison, it cost an average barge owner two hundred forty-one dollars and fifty cents to have a horse pull his barge the same distance while loaded with a hundred tons of freight. There was one design problem. The *Newman* had a seven foot draft, which was too deep for the canal. The vessel grounded more than twenty times.

Another strong contender was the *Fountain City,* designed by a man named Hunter. It also used propellers, but the wheels feathered from both quarters of the stern, directing water against the rudder. The *Fountain City, William Newman,* and other power barges like the *C. Hemje* and *William Baxter* were all competing by the end of the season, not only for the prize, but for cargo. The age of power vessels on the Erie Canal was at last a reality.

The contest generated a lot of interest, but research failed to turn up the name of the person who won the prize. There is suspicion that state officials reneged on their promise. A story that appeared in the *Detroit Daily Post* in February, 1873, said: "The commission . . . reports 'very gratifying results,' which seems to indicate great progress in solving the problem of cheap steam navigation . . . The commissioners do not award the prize, but recommend the legislature to renew the offer. Here is just where the sophistry comes in. The commissioners, we suspect, do not believe that any discovery in the art of navigation, of sufficient merit to deserve the prize, is likely to be made. Swiftness of motion in the boat and safety to the canal, or diametrically opposite requirements, are what are wanted and are what are not likely to be got so long as a floating body demands a displacement of water equal to its cubic measurement, and that will continue to be a law of physics for some time yet. Meanwhile, the necessity of the west for increasing shipping facilities is yearly outgrowing the capacity of the Erie ditch."

Smoking in Bed

At Beaver Island
On Lake Michigan
Tuesday, July 2

They said sailor George Bourisseau died in a spectacular fire that consumed his ship, the package steamer *Grace Dormer,* after he fell asleep smoking his pipe. Bourisseau was the only one to perish in the early morning blaze, although other crew members, who were asleep on the vessel, were almost caught. Captain Edward A. Bouchard and his wife Mary fled the flames stark naked and many others stumbled to Charles Wright's dock that morning wearing only their underwear or bedclothes as the fire made short work of the ship's wooden superstructure.

*The **Grace Dormer** was rebuilt as a ferry after it burned at Beaver Island, on Lake Michigan. One person died in the blaze. Institute for Great Lakes Research.*

The *Dormer* made weekly trips between Beaver Island and Mackinaw City, carrying supplies and passengers. The vessel also served as a ferry and light freight hauler between Mackinaw, Cheboygan and Duncan, Michigan. The ship was moored for the night at Wright's dock, partly loaded with a cargo that was going back to the mainland the next day. The blaze broke out at about 2:00 AM. It gained so fast that crew members had no time to think about saving the ship.

The burning vessel was cut loose from the dock and then scuttled to extinguish the flames. By then, the fire had swept the ship. Even though many people said the *Dormer* was a total wreck, it wasn't finished. Captain James Moffat of Port Huron, Michigan, an experienced salvager, bought the wreck that fall, pumped the water out of the hull and towed it home. It was rebuilt and put in service the next year as a ferry on the St. Clair River.

Surprise Shipwreck

At Waterworks Dock
Port Huron, Michigan
Friday, July 5

Capt. Horatio Jex never dreamed that he was about to lose his command. As he leaned over the rail of the scow *Hanson* the vessel seemed perfectly safe moored to Port Huron's waterworks dock. It was a few minutes before 11:00 AM on a fine Independence Day weekend. Who would have thought that danger lurked? Out on the St. Clair River, however, events were developing that would quickly change Jex's pleasant muse. The skippers of two area tugs, perhaps influenced by the holiday spirit in their own way, were racing. Their engineers were pouring on extra coal. The two powerful tugs were picking up speed on a downbound track. Approaching from the other direction was the steamer *Toledo*.

When the captain of the *Toledo* saw the two racing boats charging toward him, he ordered a course change to get out of their way. The turn ran the *Toledo* afoul of a partly submerged line from a nearby anchored schooner, which tangled with the steamer's rudder. The *Toledo* went out of control, turned sharply to port and rammed the *Hanson* amidships. The collision nearly cut the scow in two.

The *Hanson* was loaded with twelve thousand bricks. With that weight, once it had a hole in the hull, the scow sank like a rock. The crew barely escaped. Because it was still tied to the dock, the vessel was pulled on its side and capsized as it went down. It was a total loss.

The *Manitoba's* Bad Luck

On Lake Superior
At Michepecoten Island
Thursday, July 11

The bright new side-wheel steamer *Manitoba* was the pride of Canada's Beatty Line. Thus it was that the steamer's collision with Michepecoten Island was a major blow for company officials. Nobody was physically hurt, although Captain James B. Symes might have complained of serious injury to his pride.

The one-year-old *Manitoba* was on an upbound trip from Sarnia, Ontario, to Duluth, Minnesota, with general freight and about seventy-five passengers when it grounded on the rocks at about 1:00 PM. Symes said he was trying to

*The Beatty Line's new steamer **Manitoba** was damaged when it grounded at Michepecoten Island. Courtesy Institute for Great Lakes Research.*

enter Michepecoten Harbor in thick fog when the vessel jolted to a crunching stop. Examination showed that the *Manitoba* had a large gash in the hull near the bow. The passengers and crew waited two days before help arrived. The *Cumberland* was the first steamer to come along. With a few yanks the *Cumberland* succeeded in pulling the stricken steamer back into deep water. As soon as the hull cleared the rocks, water began filling the hold. It was discovered that the *Manitoba's* pumps could not keep up with the leak and the steamer would surely sink. Captain Symes drove it back into shallow water where it settled for a second time. The tugboats *E. M. Peck* and *Quayle* were sent to the scene. The hole in the *Manitoba* was covered with a large canvass and steam pumps placed on the deck to keep the water pumped out. The *Manitoba* steamed into Port Huron, Michigan under its own power about a week later and went into dry dock.

The Burning of Alpena

Alpena, Michigan
Saturday, July 12

The fire started in a barn located right behind the hotel at about 5:00 PM. It was fanned by a brisk northwest wind. Before Alpena fire fighters arrived with horses and steam pumpers the barn was aflame and the rear wall of the two-story hotel was burning. Within minutes the alarmed citizens knew the hotel also would be lost and the fire was spreading to a nearby jewelry store. As the fire grew hotter, the wind generated by the fire's demand for oxygen got stronger. It turned the town into an inferno. Burning embers flew out over the community, igniting new fires in a row of houses and business places along the south side of Second Street. The fire department could not contain the flames. The fire fiend spread with complete freedom where ever the winds carried it. Witnesses said they watched in horror as Mrs. Westbrook who operated a millinery store, died in the street in front of her store. Her son, George Westbrook, braved the fire to rescue her and was fatally burned. At least one other person perished and many people suffered burns. By the time it was over, sixty-five buildings in three and one-half blocks of the town were destroyed.

*The engineer of the propeller **Canisteo** died from injuries received during a fight with another sailor at Buffalo. Institute for Great Lakes Research.*

Death Blow at Buffalo

Aboard the propeller *Canisteo*
Buffalo harbor

The clubbing of Edward Helbing, chief engineer, during an altercation aboard the steamer *Canisteo*, turned out to be a murder, although nobody thought so when it first happened. Helbing did something to anger fireman Clarence Burroughs while the ship was docked at Buffalo, and Burroughs struck Helbing in the head with an iron bar. The exact time of this incident has been lost. A faded clipping in the *Buffalo Morning Express* on July 30 said it happened sometime in July, but no date was given.

Although Helbing was knocked senseless and confined to his cabin, medical help was never sought. Not that much could have been done to help him in 1872. The *Canisteo* steamed back to Cleveland, Ohio, where Helbing lived. There shipmates took him to his home. Helbing never recovered. When the *Canisteo* docked at Toledo one day, harbor police were waiting. They arrested Burroughs and charged him with murder.

Death Fight at Cleveland

Among the canal boats
At Cleveland, Ohio
Wednesday, July 17

When police were called they found Capt. Marvin Myers, master of the canal boat *Ensign,* lying dead in a pool of blood on the dock near the Center Street bridge. He was stabbed five times in the chest and stomach. Patrick Dougherty, steersman of the canal boat *Clayton,* was arrested for murder. Dougherty was drunk, but beyond that, police were puzzled for a while about the motive for the killing.

It was Capt. Daniel Kelso, from the canal boat *Joseph Stanley,* who shed some light on the crime. Kelso said he and Myers were drinking heavily that night and got into an argument with Dougherty. Afterward they decided to paint the words "Union Line" on the side of Dougherty's boat. There were hard feelings among canal boat operators about a deal the skippers of the *Clayton* and a few other boats made that week to haul more freight. Kelso and Myers were going from boat to boat, painting the words on the sides of some of the other offending vessels. They got in trouble when they woke Dougherty from a drunken stupor and asked him to help paint the sign on the side of Dougherty's boat. Dougherty went into a rage, got into a heated argument with Myers, and the two men agreed to go out on the dock and duke it out. The problem was that Dougherty didn't fight fair. When Myers grabbed Dougherty's shirt, Dougherty produced a knife and started stabbing.

The Big Hauls

The nature of sailors seems to be to make a contest out of everything they do. This was also true among ship owners and operators in the year 1872. While low water levels should have been putting restraints on the loads carried by individual boats, the masters, armed with larger and more powerful vessels, could not resist opportunities to set new records. The tugboat captains were busy finding unique ways to demonstrate the power of their steam powered vessels.

The powerful tugboat **Champion** *is shown with six schooners in tow on the St. Clair River in this early painting. Institute for Great Lakes Research.*

Some examples:

❱ The tug *Champion* was featured in the well-known painting reproduced above, with a tow of six barges passing Port Huron on the St. Clair River. The artist probably made his initial drawings for this picture on June 4 when the *Port Huron Daily Times* reported just such a tow passing the city. The *Champion* made the trip again on July 3 with eight barges in tow.

❱ The steamer *Antelope*, under the command of Capt. R. Ballentine, passed Detroit early in June with eight lumber barges in tow, all downbound for Buffalo. The line of ships stretched out for about a mile. The *Detroit Daily Post* said the vessels carried more than six million feet of lumber.

❱ Not to be outdone, the tug *Gladiator* made the same trip that month with eleven lumber barges trailing. The newspapers said it had to be a record number of barges, freight and weight pulled by any single tug.

❱ The new Union Company steamship *Java* made headlines in June when it carried a record load of one hundred five thousand bushels of oats from Chicago to Buffalo. The event was such a milestone that the Chicago Board of Trade came to the dock to see the vessel off with cheers and singing. The *Java* was gayly decorated with flags and festoons of ev-

*The tug **Gladiator** may have set a record when it towed eleven lumber laden barges in June, 1872. Institute for Great Lakes Research.*

ergreen on the railings. The tug that pulled this ship out of the harbor fired two six-pound guns at rapid intervals for about thirty minutes. The *Java* later broke its own record when it hauled twenty-one hundred tons of cargo consisting of twenty-five thousand bushels of corn, eighty-five thousand bushels of oats and another one hundred tons of general merchandise from Chicago to Buffalo. Somehow, with the help of a new designed hull and water-filled ballast tanks that could be pumped out on demand, the *Java* cleared all of the low water obstacles, including the St. Clair Flats, without going aground.

❱ The bark *D. P. Rhodes* in August set a new record when it left Marquette, Michigan with one thousand, one hundred and two tons of iron ore in its holds. Up to that date, it was the largest cargo ever carried by a sailing ship on the Great Lakes.

*The **Champion** was damaged by fire while moored at Detroit in 1872. Institute for Great Lakes Research.*

Fire Strikes the *Champion*

Detroit Dry Dock
Thursday, July 18

The mighty tugboat *Champion* was extensively damaged by fire while laid up for some routine maintenance at Detroit. The tug, which was in its fourth year of service, docked on the Detroit River, near the Detroit Dry Dock, to have its boilers cleaned. The crew went ashore for some time off while the work was being done. The watchman discovered a small fire that night in the hold and sounded an alarm. Workers were quick to respond and the fire was extinguished. Or so they thought. Something apparently was left smoldering somewhere, unseen. A few hours later the tug was blazing again. When fire fighters responded to a second alarm they found the flames eating their way through the ship's wooden superstructure.

Detroit fire fighters came with horse-drawn steam pumps and went to work at extinguishing the blaze. The dock workers thought they had a better idea. They pulled the one hundred thirty-four-foot vessel into the dry dock and sank it, letting the water put out the fire. The dry dock later was pumped out and the *Champion* was rebuilt. The tug continued service on the lakes until another fire destroyed it at Put-In-Bay, Ohio, on Lake Erie, in 1902.

Citizen to the Rescue

On Lake Erie
Off Long Point
Monday, July 22

    The crew of the sinking schooner *D. L. Couch* was glad when at about noon the sails of the schooner *Citizen* appeared on the horizon. The coal laden *Couch* had sprung a leak during the night. Even though the crew worked hard at the bilge pump, they could not save their ship.
    Sometime after dawn the weary sailors hoisted distress signals and prepared to launch the life boat. The *Citizen's* master, Capt. Owen Myrick, pulled his vessel alongside the sinking schooner with such skill that not one of the shipwrecked sailors got wet. The master of the *Couch* had time to rescue his papers and a few other items of value.
    The *Couch* was sunk to the decks when the *Citizen* hoisted sail and pulled away from it. The schooner sank at about 1:00 PM in about one hundred and twenty feet of water about two and one-half miles off shore.

The *Black Duck*

On Lake Ontario
Friday, July 26

    The sloop *Black Duck* was wrecked on Lake Ontario, but details about the incident are sketchy. A story in the *Buffalo Morning Express* said the *Black Duck* was bound from Sackett's Harbor to Oswego, and that the vessel went ashore in Mexico Bay on the night of July 26. Other clippings suggested that the *Black Duck* foundered in deep water. They said the ship was laden with coal, bound the other way from Oswego to Dexter, New York, on Sackett's Harbor at the far eastern end of the lake. The story in the *Morning Express* said the captain, his wife, and one deck hand, came ashore in a punt. The open boat apparently capsized in the surf because the captain's wife almost drowned. No names were given.

The Burning of the *Mary Robinson*

At the Straits of Mackinac
Near Skellagailee Light
Monday, July 29

They said it was faulty construction that caused the fire that swept the new Canadian steam barge *Mary R. Robinson*. The second engineer said an earlier fire had been extinguished in a wooden bulkhead located too close to the boiler. This engineer, who remained anonymous, said he reported the problem to Canadian authorities, but nothing was done. He said the bulkhead was only eight inches from the boiler, which was inviting trouble. He was not surprised when the *Mary Robinson* caught fire a second time, on its second trip. This time the ship was turned into a burned-out smoldering wreck. Fortunately, nobody was hurt.

The steamer was carrying wheat from Chicago to Collingwood, Ontario, and had the schooner *New Dominion* in tow when the fire was discovered at about 10:00 PM when off Skellagailee. The crew turned their attention to fighting the fire until they were driven from the engine room. By then it was too late for anyone to shut down the engines, and this was a mistake. Capt. J. McPherson said the ship was moving full speed against the wind, which helped fan the flames. He said all attempts to battle the fire on the deck were fruitless. The racing engines also made it impossible for the crew to escape in the ship's life boat.

After the fire burned away the tow line to the trailing schooner, the blazing steamer galloped away from the *New Dominion*. The coals that fed the fires in the boiler finally began to cool and the engines slowed down enough to allow the crew to make a get-away. They said they almost didn't make it. Some of the men had the hairs on their head singed. The *New Dominion* took everybody on board after it caught up with the life boat. In the meantime, the propeller *City of Fremont* was moored at nearby LaCrosse Village, taking on wood, and saw the fire. Captain Starkweather took his ship out to offer assistance. The wrecking tug *Leviathan* found the burned out wreck aground in Hog Island Bay. The hull was towed to Toronto. Plans were to rebuild it.

The Old Steamer Burns

On The Saginaw River
Wednesday, August 7

    The side-wheeler *Ajax* caught fire while anchored at Stone Island on Wednesday night. Nobody was aboard the ship or around the dock so the fire got a good start before it was discovered. The *Ajax* was an old vessel and they said it wasn't worth much. The fire was hardly mentioned in the newspapers in Michigan that week. A thirty-year-old rotting steamer burning at its wharf in 1872 wasn't worth much ink. One writer remembered that the ship was used as a tugboat for several years, probably bringing lumber rafts down the river to Bay City. The *Saginaw Daily Courier* said the *Ajax* was handy because its shallow draft allowed the vessel to travel streams where other ships feared to go.

Fearless Frenzy

Off the Door Peninsula
On Lake Michigan
Thursday, August 8

    The schooner *Fearless* was heavily laden with lumber, its sails billowing before the wind on a trip to Milwaukee, when the center board box started leaking. The crew was summoned from their bunks early in the morning after water was discovered in the hold. Everybody took turns on the bilge pumps, but the sailors could not keep ahead of the rising water. Before long the ship was waterlogged and out of control. After a while it turned into the seas and capsized. The sailors struggled in the water for a while until someone cut away the lifeboat. After scrambling in the boat the men pulled for the Wisconsin coast. Somewhere near Whitefish Point, the brig *Commerce* found them and took everybody to Manitowoc. A tug found the *Fearless* still floating upside down on August 12, and towed it to Milwaukee. The ship was severely damaged. The fore and main sails were gone, as was the flying jib, the hatches, running lines, blocks, masts and the cabin roof.

STEAMBOATS IN ICE

*Fire caused extensive damage to the tug **Danforth** at Duluth harbor. Institute for Great Lakes Research.*

Sinking a Burning Tug

At Duluth, Minnesota
Friday, August 9

A passing train crew noticed fire on the moored tugboat *F. L. Danforth* just before 3:00 AM and the Duluth Fire Department was called. The fifty-eight-foot long tug was tied at the Duluth dock, nudging close under the bow of the schooner *Saginaw* and only a few hundred feet away from one of the city's big grain elevators. Fire fighters knew they had to work fast to keep the fire from turning into a major conflagration.

Some fast-thinking dock workers tried to fight the blaze in their own unique way before the fire department arrived. They cut the *Danforth* loose and with the help of another harbor tug, pulled it up against the breakwater next to a rock-filled scow moored on the west side of the breakwater. The scow was in place for a wall refurbishing project. The workers foolishly thought that by piling enough rocks on the deck of the blazing boat, they could sink the *Danforth* and put out the fire. It was a terrible idea. Because tugboats often have to stand up against extreme weather, their hulls are designed

75

with high sideboards that resist sinking. The Duluth welldoers devoted much time and energy tossing rocks and boulders into the tug's open deck but the *Danforth* would not sink. When they saw the lights and realized that the Duluth Fire Department was at the dock, they towed the burning *Danforth* back into the harbor so fire fighters could put out the blaze the normal way, with fire hoses and water.

The fire was out by 4:30 AM, but by then the tug was severely damaged. The charred hull was left chained to the dock. The next morning the *Danforth* was sunk in seven feet of water. The rocks finally did their job. The wreck was raised and rebuilt that fall. It continued to sail the lakes until it burned and sank at Superior, Wisconsin, in 1892, twenty years later.

A Sitting Duck

On Lake Michigan
Off Manitowoc, Wisconsin
Friday, August 16

Sailing ships in 1872 were not equipped with auxiliary diesel engines to keep them moving when the wind stopped blowing. When the wind failed early on Friday, Captain Torrison found his schooner *Josephine Lawrence* becalmed on Lake Michigan, a few miles off the Wisconsin coast.

Torrison and his crew waited patiently for the weather to change. It did. A dense fog developed, hiding the schooner from view of passing ships. This only added to Torrison's frustration. He realized that his ship now was a sitting duck, waiting to be hit by one of the many steamships sharing the lake that morning. The steamers were not stopped by the whims of wind. The sun came up and began beating down on the fog. It was shortly after 7:00 AM and Torrison was optimistic now that his luck would change. It did. He was jarred by the nearby blast of an approaching steamship. The *Lawrence's* sails were still set, in hopes of catching the slightest breeze, and Torrison said he heard men on the deck of the steamer shout that they could see the topmasts of a schooner dead ahead. He heard two strokes of the steamer's bell, which made him believe his ship was seen and that the steamer

STEAMBOATS IN ICE

would turn away. Torrison shouted into the gloom, pleading with the wheelsman to turn the steamer because he was becalmed and unable to get out of the way.

To his horror, Torrison said he saw the upper works of the steamship come out of the fog and it was on a collision course. It was the propeller *Favorite* that appeared. The ship hit the *Lawrence* on the port quarter, about ten feet forward of the wheel. The collision came with such force the wooden schooner immediately capsized. The crew of the *Lawrence* survived the accident. They were pulled from the water by the *Favorite*. The *Lawrence*, which was a wooden ship loaded with lumber, didn't sink. It floated on its beam ends for a day until a tug towed it into Manitowoc.

Killed by Lightning

On Lake Michigan
Wednesday, August 14

The crew of the three-masted schooner *Day Spring* learned that lightning, indeed, can strike twice, and with deadly accuracy. The ship was crossing Lake Michigan with a load of wood bound for Milwaukee when a severe electrical

*One sailor died and a second man was hurt when lightning struck the schooner **Day Spring** on Lake Michigan. Institute for Great Lakes Research.*

storm developed. As the swirling black clouds bore down on the schooner, Captain Miller had a wary eye on the sky. Because he thought there might be strong wind, he called the entire crew to the deck.

Sailors Tobian Tobielson, of Fickkefjord, Norway, and F. Mueller, of Sheboygan, Wisconsin, were among them. They weren't busy at the moment so they were watching the storm while sitting on a barrel of tar under the foremast. The sailors were startled when a bolt of lightning hit the deck a few feet away. Miller began shouting a warning to the two men to get out from under the mast. Before he got the words out of his mouth, a second bolt struck the mast and knocked both Tobielson and Mueller to the deck. Tobielson was killed instantly. Mueller was stunned for several hours but he survived. His right arm was burned and blistered. The lightning shattered the topmast, melted the iron at the top, and burned a groove six inches wide down the length of the mast.

Lake Breeze Fire

On Lake Huron
Off Au Sable, Michigan
Monday, August 26

The propeller *Lake Breeze* was steaming from Saginaw to Mackinaw City with freight and about forty passengers when fire broke out in the cook room. The alarm was sounded and all hands scrambled to fight the flames. Capt. M. S. Lathrop was determined to save his ship. He ordered the engines shut down to reduce any extra draft created by the moving ship. He also wanted to divert all of the steam power to the pumps to get as much water flowing through them to the fire as possible.

The sailors battled smoke and flames for several anxious moments while passengers huddled in frightened groups, wondering if they would ever see port or home again. Finally, the word spread through the ship that the fire was out. The *Lake Breeze* was saved. Everybody breathed easier. The partially burned ship was still smoking when it arrived at Mackinaw City that night, but the *Lake Breeze* was still afloat and the passengers were alive and well.

Fire on the *Bertschy*

De Pere, Wisconsin
Sunday, August 25

It was a warm summer evening. The steamer *J. Bertschy* was moored at the Iron Company dock along the river at De Pere, and Captain Vance was on the deck, enjoying the evening. The mate was there too, and they were talking. The ship had just arrived from Lake Superior with its holds laden with iron ore. Workers were preparing to start unloading.

The routine was shattered at about eight o'clock when a crew member ran on deck and announced a fire in the after hold. Vance sounded an alarm and ordered his crew to work, running out fire hoses and directing steam from the boiler to the pump that sent water surging through the lines. Someone also called the De Pere Fire Department, which, it turned out, was a very good idea.

Even before fire fighting efforts got organized, smoke and flames were seen breaking through the aft hatches. Within minutes, the fire was spreading through the wooden cabins on the deck. The *Bertschy's* crew was driven back by the progressing flames, and things were looking bad. The tide was turned, however, when the De Pere fire fighters arrived with another steam pump. Within a few minutes the fire was driven back, and eventually the fire was out.

The *J. Bertschy* was saved, but the stern cabins were severely damaged. The fire also damaged the engine room.

"Oh Lord, Have Mercy..."

On Lake Michigan
Near Pentwater, Michigan
Wednesday, August 28

School was starting early for Robert West, the eight-year-old son of Capt. Frank R. West, master of the new schooner *Louis Meeker*. Young West and a friend, Edward Erickson, were traveling as special guests aboard the *Meeker* on a trip from Chicago to Buffalo. The schooner was laden with wheat. Having two bright-eyed boys aboard, watching everything that was going on, was an exhilarating experience at first for Captain West and his crew. West saw the trip as an opportunity to introduce his son to the ways of the sea, perhaps with thoughts of someday encouraging young Robert to follow in his father's shoes. Who knows, the boy might one day become master of his own ship, the captain dared to think. The rest of the crew thought that having the boys on board was a pleasant change in the everyday routine.

Things were not going as well as West had hoped. Instead of a perfect run, scudding romantically before brisk southwesterly winds, the *Meeker* was next to becalmed from the moment it left Chicago on August 24. The winds were so light, the ship had every inch of sail set. Even at that, the *Meeker* was creeping so slowly up the Michigan shoreline, it was not quite off Pentwater on Wednesday morning, four days later. Things were so bad, the men were losing their patience. Tempers flared. Instead of seeing the romantic side of the sea, the boys were witnessing the drudgery of waiting. Captain West was hoping something would change soon. He got his wish, but it wasn't what he expected.

A few light rain showers developed during the night and by dawn West noticed that the sky looked unsettled. A weather front was approaching. That usually meant squalls with lots of wind. He ordered the sails taken in as a precaution. At about 10:00 AM a storm rolled across the lake with great speed from the southwest. All sails were reefed and the crew was busy buttoning down the ship when the wind hit. It came with such power that even though it hit bare masts, it capsized the ship.

First mate Charles R. Davis said he was just stepping out on the deck when the squall hit. He said he passed the captain's son on the stairs. As the ship started to go over, Davis said he ran toward the stern to cut away the fall to the life boat. He didn't get there in time and rode the ship over on its side. He said Captain West was on the foredeck when the ship capsized. West shouted: "Oh, Lord, have mercy on me," before he sank out of sight. He never came up again.

Davis said the *Meeker* remained for about fifteen minutes on its beam ends, with the hatches about two-thirds of the way under water, before it sank. Young Robert West and three sailors were trapped below deck and they went down with the ship. The other three were identified as E. Nelson, Frank Barker and the ship's steward, whose name was not given. The remainder of the crew was left struggling in the water. Peter Danielson, the second mate, dove to try to cut away the lifeboat, and almost died there. When the *Meeker* sank, Danielson was drawn with it into deep water. He held his breath until he made it back to the surface.

Davis said he cut the ship's mizzen gaff adrift and then hung on that. Two other sailors joined him. The other crew members, identified as Danielson, Halver Thompson, Andrew Harts, John Ryng plus Robert West's traveling friend, Edward Erickson, were still alive when they were picked up by the schooner *William O. Brown* at about 4:00 PM.

Stuck in the Mud

In the flats near Muskegon, Michigan
Along the Lake Michigan coast
Thursday, August 29

The low water left many stray logs piled up in the shallows along the Muskegon River and on the coast of Lake Michigan. The old paddle-wheel-powered tug *Monitor* was busy rounding up floating logs while nearby Fred Figge was working with a team of oxen, pulling logs out of the mud.

The wind was up this day and the *Monitor* got pushed into some water that wasn't water at all . . . just mud with a watery looking surface. The vessel got stuck in the mud. The captain raised steam and the big wheel turned, scooping the ooze and then throwing it in large globs through the air on both sides of the boat. But even with its shallow draft, which made the *Monitor* the perfect vessel for the work it was doing, it could not pull free again.

The crew got down in the mud and pushed, while the wheel still churned. Mud flew and everybody got plastered with it. But the old tugboat remained fast. Finally Figge brought his oxen around. He hooked them to the steamer and told them to pull. The beasts dragged the *Monitor* right back into deep water.

Late Summer Blow

The schooner *Erie* was loaded with coal, on a trip from Cleveland to Detroit, when it ran into rough weather on Lake Erie. Capt. John L. Andres knew the ship was ripe after thirty-nine years on the lakes, so he dropped anchor Thursday night, August 29, off Kelleys Island, where the *Erie* had some shelter. That night a full-fledged storm developed and the schooner took a terrible beating. Water flooded the hold. The crew worked the bilge pumps, but they could not save the old ship. The *Erie* sank at its anchors at about 1:00 AM. The crew escaped in the life boat. The shipwrecked sailors were later rescued by the passing propeller *Huron City* and taken to Sandusky, Ohio. Some said the *Erie* was among the oldest vessels on the lakes. It was built in 1833 and at one time served as a U.S. revenue cutter.

The storm that sank the *Erie* caused havoc for several other ships:

▶ The Canadian brig *Ocean*, commanded by Captain Dunn, sprang a leak in rough weather on Lake Erie while carrying stone from Cleveland, Ohio, to Picton, Ontario. The ship sank fifteen minutes after the leak was discovered. Seven sailors narrowly escaped in the yawl boat. The vessel sank about thirty miles out of port.

▶ The schooner *G. J. Whitney* went ashore at Vermillion, Ohio, on Lake Erie, and sank with a load of block stone. The wrecking steamer *Magnet* pulled this hard-luck ship (see index) free a few days later after one hundred twenty tons of stone were removed to a lighter.

▶ The schooner *Orion*, loaded with stone from Cleveland, foundered off Lake Erie's Long Point. The crew escaped in the ship's yawl but could not make land on the Canadian side of the lake. The boat was blown away from shore, so the sailors pulled hard for the American coast, arriving the next day near Dunkirk, New York.

❯ The schooner *Richardson* went aground at Lake Huron's Presque Isle. The crew escaped.

❯ The barge *St. Clair* waterlogged at the southern end of Lake Huron. The vessel was lumber laden and under tow. Part of the deck load washed away. The barge remained afloat until it reached Port Huron, then sank at the dock. The *St. Clair* later was raised and towed to Detroit for repair.

❯ The schooners *Montank* and *Pathfinder* went ashore at Point Edward, also at the southern end of Lake Huron. The bark *City of Buffalo* ran aground on the St. Clair River. All three vessels waited for tugs to help pull them free.

❯ When the schooner *Maxwell* grounded in the St. Clair Flats, the barge in tow behind the *Maxwell*, the *David Steward*, rammed the *Maxwell's* stern. The collision cut a large hole in the *Maxwell's* hull and shoved the ship's cabin forward. The *Maxwell* was a sorry mess when it was towed into Fitzgerald's dry dock at Port Huron the next day.

❯ The propeller *City of Madison* ran into the storm on Lake Superior after leaving Marquette with a load of pig iron. When the cargo shifted, the *Madison* returned to Marquette to get it rearranged. On a second try, the cargo shifted again, forcing the *Madison* to return yet again, this time with some structural damage.

❯ The steamer *City of London* was in the middle of Lake Ontario, on route from London to Toledo, when the storm came. The wind drove the steamer to the Canadian shore where it sought refuge in the Genesee River. The *London* tossed about so badly that the cargo and cabin furnishings were damaged.

STEAMBOATS IN ICE

Capt. Henry Bundy

Gospel Ship

When Capt. Henry Bundy brought his tidy little schooner *Glad Tidings* into ports along the Great Lakes during the 1870s, he always drew attention. Bundy's vessel was well known as the traveling gospel ship. His cargo was the Bible from which he preached to sailors from the docks or in empty warehouses . . . wherever he found room. His reputation followed him up and down the lakes. He became well known from Chicago north to Duluth and east to Buffalo. Newspaper editors sometimes joked about Bundy, while other writers honored him with words of praise. His story is one of personal sacrifice and dedication, which began with Bundy's deliverance from a storm.

Bundy was a native of England who began a career as a sailor on the high seas before coming to the United States and taking a job on the lakes. He was a hard worker and skilled sailor who soon became the master of the schooner *Potomac*. One day the *Potomac* was caught in a late November gale on Lake Erie. As he tried to bring the ship into Cleveland harbor, a giant wave turned the vessel off course and the hull slammed against the outside of the breakwater. There the *Potomac* was in danger of being dashed to pieces. As the waves thundered over the decks, Bundy realized that he and his crew were in serious trouble. They could do nothing to save either the ship or themselves. With nowhere else to turn, Bundy started praying. As he asked for deliverance a large wave swept the deck and carried everyone over the breakwater. They found themselves alive and swimming in calm water. Bundy and his crew survived. Even the *Potomac* was salvaged and repaired. Bundy was deeply moved. He spent the winter at Chicago, attending prayer meetings. The next spring he made a decision to dedicate the rest of his life to God's service.

He said God spoke to him in the cabin of his ship while it was docked at Chicago, waiting for a tug to tow it into Lake Michigan. The voice instructed him to "leave the ship." To the astonishment of the crew, Bundy did just that. He went home to his wife and waited for something to happen. He told her that "if the Lord commanded me to do this, He will take care of me." A few days later Bundy took a job at the seaman's bethel, serving sailors while they were in port. Bundy could not read or write but it was during this time that he found a tutor, and gained these key skills. He stayed in Chicago five years, attending church, reading his Bible and preparing for the amazing ministry that followed. Then he bought his first gospel ship, a small schooner which he named *Glad Tidings*. It was with that vessel that Bundy started a ministry to Great Lakes sailors that has been unparalleled before or since.

Bundy recognized a need for a traveling evangelist to visit the seaport towns and lumber camps he had been associated with. He set sail from Chicago with two ordained ministers aboard, with plans to do missionary work on Beaver Island. On the way a storm drove his ship to shelter at Sheboygan, Wisconsin. It was a serious storm and people marveled that the little schooner survived it. Bundy and the other men saw this as an opportunity to start their ministry. They began preaching to the people on the dock. This became the pattern of his ministry from that day on. Bundy became known all over the lakes as the itinerant preacher on the gospel ship.

Some newspapers poked good natured fun at Bundy's venture. The *Duluth Daily News* on June 10, 1890, said: "Captain Bundy's gospel ship *'Glad Tidings'* is coming up to Duluth. The unregenerate dockwalloper will please to brace up." For the most part, the writers of the day seemed to respect and even endorse what Bundy was doing. The *Chicago Inter Ocean* described Bundy in 1876 as "an energetic, active man" who has "a will of his own and nothing discourages him . . . certainly not the jeers of a few reprobates and unbelievers who cannot appreciate the fact that a man like the captain can preach Christ and not be a hypocrite, with some sinister design behind." Bundy was described as a short, stout, thickset man, who was slightly bald. One writer said he had a "very pleasing appearance."

His little schooner sailed each summer from port to port. Bundy preached to fishermen, sailors, mill hands and all types of dock workers and laborers. In 1877, a Chicago newspaper reporter attended one of Bundy's "divine services" held in a lumber market and gave the following report: "The Rev. Captain Bundy preached one of his blunt, earnest sermons, on this occasion, taking the text 'The Water of Life,' and there was the usual vigorous singing from strong lungs. Few were present when the captain commenced his discourse, but they came one by one and in groups of two and three until there was quite a large congregation." The writer said Bundy "does not command beautiful language. He is an educated, intelligent man, however, and talks straight to the point. His undying faith and evident earnestness have great effect on his hearers. Meeting after meeting we have seen scoffers stand in the assemblage before him for no other purpose than to catch an opportunity . . . an appropriate place . . . for catcalls, and we have seen these same scoffers realize their own degradation and quietly edge away or stand attentive listeners until the last word was uttered. These lumber market meetings, inaugurated by Captain Bundy several years ago, have done much good."

Some said Bundy seemed to live a charmed life. Believers said he traveled under God's protection. Although caught in some serious gales, the *Glad Tidings* almost always sailed unharmed into port amid the wreckage of larger, stouter vessels that failed. The ship grounded a few times, but there is no record of serious damage. A terrible northeaster swept the lakes in early November, 1877, leaving many vessels wrecked. Yet in the midst of the horror stories about the storm, there appeared a clipping in the *Chicago Inter Ocean* about Bundy's gospel ship arriving at Chicago following a long cruise on Lake Michigan. The newspaper said the ship "looks as well as she did when she left here."

Bundy's first vessels were quite small. The original *Glad Tidings* was replaced in 1877 by a forty-foot long schoo-

STEAMBOATS IN ICE

One of Capt. Henry Bundy's sailing Gospel Ships **Glad Tidings** *moored at Lake Erie's Kelley's Island. This was probably Bundy's third ship. Institute for Great Lakes Research.*

ner, which indicated that the first one must have been about the size of a modern pleasure boat. Bundy owned two other vessels after that. *Glad Tidings III* was a one hundred and thirteen-foot long schooner, and *Glad Tidings IV* was a seventy-foot long steamer. He continued his shoreline ministry until ill health drove him back to Chicago. The last *Glad Tidings* was sold in 1896 to a man in St. Ignace, Michigan, who put the vessel in service as the *Elva*. Bundy continued his ministry in Chicago for several years after that. At first, Bundy was self ordained. He preached during the early years without the authority of churchdom. He was officially ordained by the First Congregational Church in June, 1878, in Farwell Hall, Chicago.

Bundy died on September 15, 1906, at the age of 80 at his home in Chicago. He was the father of a son, Henry T. Bundy, and two daughters, Agnes Bundy and Mrs. E. E. Scott.

STEAMBOATS IN ICE

Storms of Autumn

September 1 - October 31

STEAMBOATS IN ICE

STEAMBOATS IN ICE

*The **R. G. Crawford** was struck by lightning while anchored off Long Point. Institute for Great Lakes Research.*

They Lost Their Nerve

Under Long Point
Lake Erie
Thursday, September 5

    The thunderstorm raked a fleet of sailing ships anchored to the lee of Long Point that afternoon. The storm was violent, but the lakers were riding it out. Then, without warning, a bolt of lightning split the foremast on the schooner *R. C. Crawford*, causing the reefed sails, rigging and ropes to crash to the deck in a cloud of smoke. The watchman was thrown to the deck when the bolt hit the foremast. He wasn't badly hurt. The strike cut a wedge through the foremast to the deck, tore the braces from their places, scattered coal in the hold and raised up part of the deck as if there had been an explosion.

As they came on deck to assess the damage, the crew of the *Crawford* noticed the sailors in a nearby vessel, the schooner *Hippogriffe*, launching the ship's lifeboat and pulling frantically through the rain for shore. Query later turned up the reason. The *Hippogriffe* was loaded with gunpowder.

The *Sargent* is Missing!

At Detroit, Michigan
Friday, September 6

Nine days after it set sail from Port Colborne, bound for Detroit with a load of pig iron, word was received that something may have happened to the schooner *J. W. Sargent*. The seventeen-year-old ship was overdue at Detroit and the crews of ships arriving from Lake Erie ports said they hadn't seen a sign of it. By September 6 the Detroit newspapers were suggesting that the *Sargent* was another victim of the storm of August 29, which hit one day after the ship left Port Colborne. People who knew Capt. William Simms were beginning to express regrets about his death. They said Simms was traveling with his wife and their adopted son, and that the *Sargent* was carrying a crew of four other men.

That afternoon the *Sargent* arrived at Detroit. Simms said the late arrival was, indeed, caused by the storm. He said the blow hit the ship off Round Eau, and he ran southwest with the wind for shelter at Erie, Pennsylvania. He said he laid over at Erie for a few days, and sent a telegraph to the owners about his location. The word was never relayed to Detroit where people were waiting for the *Sargent's* arrival.

The *Sargent* was really lost on Lake Erie three months later. It was caught in a November storm, got wedged in the ice off Middle Sister Island, then sank during the winter. The crew escaped. The story appears later in this book.

Where There is Smoke...

Aboard the *L. B. Sheppard*
On Lake Michigan
Sometime early in September

Captain Calloway, master of the schooner *L. B. Sheppard*, fancied he smelled something burning not long after his boat set sail from Escanaba, Michigan. When he checked the cargo hold, Calloway discovered, to his horror, that his command was very close to destruction by fire.

The *Sheppard's* cargo for that trip included brick, barrels of quick lime and twelve tons of hay, stored on top of the brick and lime. Down deep in the hold, under the hay, Calloway found that a barrel of lime had become wet and was smoldering. Quick lime gets hot when exposed to water. When confined inside a wooden barrel, it can generate enough heat to start a fire. The hay had to be removed before the heated lime barrel could be removed and thrown overboard.

Calloway said it was a close call. The crew worked feverishly digging that smoldering time bomb from the hold, knowing that at any moment it could ignite the hay and subsequently torch the ship. They won the race and the *Sheppard* was saved.

Striking for a Better Way

The movement didn't get very well organized. Still, all around the Great Lakes workers were grumbling about the wages they were receiving for the work they did. Sailors, miners and lumbermen were all doing dangerous work, staying on the job for long, hard hours, but earning an average of two dollars and fifty cents an hour. Sailors struck the boats for better pay at both ends of the lakes at almost the same time. It happened on Tuesday, September 10 at Chicago and the very next day in Buffalo. The Chicago strikers said they would not sail during the dangerous fall season at their regular rate of pay. Because of the danger of the autumn gales, they said they wanted three dollars before they left port. While they raised a fuss for a few days, the effort failed. The number of strikers was small, and they never got the support of the majority of sailors.

At Buffalo, the sailors were visited on various moored vessels by gangs of men who urged them to go on strike. They said they were trying to get wages up on some ships from one dollar and seventy-five cents to two dollars and fifty cents a day. The visitors persuaded some of the men to join the strike until the police arrived and broke up the crowds. The walkout at Buffalo generated a small amount of success, however. Sailors walked off their jobs from the schooners *Mary E. Jones, D. P. Dobbins* and *John Minor*. Capt. M. Galligan, master of the *Jones,* asked harbor authorities to force the workers back to work aboard his boat because he said they signed contracts to work for the wages they were getting. A story in the *Buffalo Morning Express* said some captains were forced to pay the higher wages so they could get their vessels out of port that week.

Lumber workers struck the mills at Bay City at or about July 1 for better working conditions. They said they wanted ten hour working days instead of twelve.

Erie Horror Story

Off Rondeau, Ontario
On Lake Erie
Friday, September 13

When Morris Flynn, first mate of the schooner *Paragon,* took two other sailors in a small boat to investigate some wreckage floating off Rondeau, he found something so gruesome he first had to look away. There, still strapped to the rail of a capsized wreck, were the bodies of seven men. Fortunately, Flynn didn't turn away even though the seas were high and it seemed at first that there was nothing he or the crew of the *Paragon* could do to help these sailors. Closer inspection revealed a miracle. One of the seven men in the boat was still alive! James Low, first mate of the wrecked schooner *Rapid* was taken aboard the *Paragon* that afternoon in an unconscious condition. His hands and face were so swollen he was first thought dead. He remained in a coma for hours. Low recovered to tell his story which was printed in the *Toledo Blade* on September 21. Low said he was in the water for sixty hours, from the time the *Rapid* capsized in a gale at midnight Friday until he was rescued about noon on Monday. He said the *Rapid* left the Union Dock on Pigeon Bay, Ontario, with five thousand railroad ties bound for Buffalo. That the ship sailed on a Friday, something many superstitious sailors believed brought bad luck, was never mentioned by Low. What was worse, it was an especially risky day for any vessel to have set sail because it was Friday the 13th! These things probably crossed the mind of Capt. Andrew Henderson, the *Rapid's* master, many times before he died.

The *Rapid's* troubles came up fast. As the storm developed, Captain Henderson decided to turn the boat around and try to reach Rondeau, or some other safe anchorage until things blew over. The schooner capsized while turning. Most of the crew members were on the deck when it happened and they ended up in the water clinging to the overturned ship. He said the cook, Annie Brown, was trapped below deck in her cabin and drowned right away. The cabin later washed away with Brown's body still inside.

The seven other crew members, Captain Henderson, Low, Fred Taylor, Alex McLeod, Daniel O'Brien, Alphonso Fayette and Michael McCaffrey, strapped themselves to the rail and waited for a passing vessel to find them. Low said the cold wait was unbearable. The ship remained on its side, waterlogged and sunk low in the water. Heavy seas continually swept over the men so they did not dare to fall asleep for fear of being drowned. There was no food. After a while, the ship started breaking up. He said he remembered the ties breaking through the deck and floating away. The sailors waited and waited but rescue eluded them. The hours passed slowly. Then the days and nights. The sailors began dying on Sunday. Low said Captain Henderson was the first to go. After that, the others slipped away. Low was in a coma and close to death when he was found. He didn't realize he was saved until he woke up in somebody's bed.

Philo S. Bemis

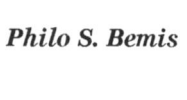

Burning Bemis

On Lake Huron
Near Alpena, Mich.
Sunday, September 15

The tug *Philo S. Bemis* was out on Lake Huron early, steaming from Alpena to Nine Mile Point to pick up a raft of logs for a tow south. The trip was never finished. When off Plough's Fishery, six miles from Alpena, a fire was discovered in the hold under the boilers. Before anybody could lift a finger to fight it, the blaze spread to a stack of pine slabs stored in the hold as fuel for the trip. Once the slabs took fire, the blaze was too hot and too fierce for anybody to extinguish.

Capt. E. M. Harrington turned the tug toward shore, about two miles away, so he and his two-member crew would have an easier escape. Before the vessel got far, however, the fire spread to a deck load of pine slabs, and the boat turned into a blazing inferno. The three men fled in the life boat.

A brisk offshore wind blew the *Bemis* ashore where it burned until it sank in three feet of water. Although extensively damaged, the record shows that the *Bemis* was raised and rebuilt. The vessel remained on the lakes until 1879.

Saving the *W. H. Hawkins*

On Lake Michigan
Off Grand Haven, Michigan
Wednesday, September 17

    The schooner *W. H. Hawkins,* under the command of Captain Baggs, sprang a serious leak early Wednesday morning during stormy weather when it was about twenty-five miles southwest of Grand Haven. The crew manned the pumps but the water gained. Soon the wooden ship, laden with lumber, waterlogged and became unmanageable. The crew started throwing the cargo overboard, hoping to save the ship and, if lucky, themselves. The situation was getting serious when, about dawn, Capt. Henry Bundy's gospel ship *Glad Tidings,* came along and took all eight members of the crew and a lone passenger aboard. Captain Baggs said the seas were still high and he praised Bundy's seamanship. He said Bundy put the *Glad Tidings* at risk to save the stranded sailors.
    The *Glad Tidings* later arrived at Muskegon, Michigan, where the word spread that the *Hawkins* was a floating wreck. The tug *Alice* that evening brought the *Hawkins* into Grand Haven. There it was pumped out and repaired.

Riding in on a Wheelhouse

On Lake Erie
Near Port Burwell, Ontario
Wednesday, September 18

    The lumber barges *Forester* and *R. R. Elliott* stranded and went to pieces, and a third barge, the *Bay City*, waterlogged and for a time was feared lost when they were caught together in a storm. That all three crews escaped alive was good news. The barges were in a string, all loaded with lumber and making their way behind the steamer-barge *Dunkirk* from Bay City, Michigan, to Tonawanda, New York when the storm developed on Lake Erie. Captain Eastman, master of the *Bay City*, said the *Elliott* and *Forester* both became waterlogged and unmanageable when the vessels were about fifteen miles off Port Burwell. Captain Murdock, skipper of the *Dunkirk,* turned toward the Canadian shore the moment he knew the vessels were in trouble. He hoped to get on the lee side of Long Point. As the two barges sank deeper and deeper in the water, they acted like sea anchors, pulling against the thrust of the *Dunkirk's* engines. As the storm intensified, the *Dunkirk* cut the line to all three barges when about eight miles from shore and saved itself from the gale.

Eastman said the *Bay City* dropped anchor and rode out the storm. The anchor held, and the barge turned into the wind. He said the heavy seas tore at the barge until they started carrying away the deck load of lumber lashed to the bow. As the bow of the ship lightened, the lumber still stacked at the stern of the *Bay City* caused the rear of the ship to drop lower in the water. The boat flooded and became partly sunk. It became a dangerous and very uncomfortable place for the crew. Eastman told the sailors they were free to take the yawl boat and try to get to shore. Everybody left except Eastman and one unnamed sailor, who agreed to stay aboard to help. The *Dunkirk* returned a day or two later and towed the *Bay City* on to Tonawanda, New York, where the remaining lumber was taken off and the hull was pumped out.

Meanwhile the crews of the *Elliott* and *Forester* were also in trouble. Their ships already were waterlogged. If anchors were dropped, they did not hold. Both vessels stranded and started breaking up in the storm. The crew of the *Elliott* went ashore in the lifeboat, but the crew of the *Forester* chose a more unconventional way of escape. Just before they left the ship, a large wave tore off the wheelhouse, dropping it upside down in the water, close to the side of the *Forester.* This wheelhouse was made with an unusual conical design. Some said it resembled a bee hive. For some reason the crew of the *Forester* climbed inside the overturned wheelhouse and rode it to shore, instead of using a lifeboat. Perhaps something happened to the boat. Captain Murdock, three other men, the woman cook and her child, all were passengers for this strange ride. They said the wheelhouse made a perfect vehicle in the storm. The tapered sides protected them from the wind and waves, and the shape of the thing caught the wind, so it skimmed along on the surface of the lake with unexpected speed. In fact, it passed the crew of the *Bay City* who started rowing for shore ahead of the *Forester's* crew. The sailors were surprised to see Captain Murdock and his crew skudding along before the wind in their strange contraption, and making no apparent effort on their own to push it. The wheelhouse reached shore about thirty minutes ahead of the *Bay City's* life boat.

Both the *Forester* and *Elliott* had earlier, more colorful histories as steamers on the Detroit River. Both were built in 1854. The *Elliott* was a busy tugboat at Detroit, while the *Forester* carried passengers and freight between Detroit and Port Huron. Both had been side-wheelers before they were stripped of their engines and turned into barges for the ever hungry lumber trade.

Other Storm Casualties

The gale that wrecked the *Elliott* and *Forester* was nasty enough to have jostled several other vessels around. Following is a list of events:

▶ The propeller *Mendota* arrived on September 19 in Buffalo, New York, with a tow of lumber barges that showed the effects of the storm. The barge *Nellie McGlivra* lost its deck load and was waterlogged. Another barge was lost for a while on Lake Erie, but it was recovered by the tug *Frank Perew*.

▶ The propeller *Annie L. Craig* lost five lumber barges in its tow above Long Point. They were the *Barter, Braley, Ontario, Lillie May* and *Mariner*. The barges all were found safely afloat, and towed into various ports by passing boats.

▶ The scow *Louisa*, laden with bark, became waterlogged and capsized in Lake Huron off Kincaridine, Ontario. The crew was rescued after the wreck drifted ashore.

▶ The scow *A. Baker*, loaded with stone, went ashore at Cedar Point, Ohio.

▶ The schooner *Sweet Home*, sailing from Clayton, New York, to Kingston, Ontario, sank in the St. Lawrence River.

▶ The schooner *Midnight* went aground on Hog Island Reef in the Straits of Mackinac.

Capsized

On Lake St. Clair
Monday, September 23

Teenagers Frank and George Walters left their Detroit home for an adventurous trip on the Detroit River. They rented a small skiff which was equipped with oars and a small sail, and told friends they were taking a trip up the river to Belle Isle. Whether by design or whim, when they reached the island, they didn't stop. By 4:00 PM their little boat was on Lake St. Clair, whisking briskly along before a fresh breeze.

The Walters were not experienced sailors. Eighteen-year-old Frank and George, his younger brother by two years, took the little craft about a mile out into the lake before deciding to turn around for the ride home. A gust of wind capsized the boat and the boys found themselves in the water beside an overturned boat. Fortunately, both boys could swim and they knew one basic rule of safety. They stayed with their boat. They held on and waited for help. No vessels came near and the wind blew them farther and farther out into the lake. They were still there when the sun went down.

By now, the boys were desperate. They were exhausted, cold and hungry, and the prospect of spending all night in the water, clinging to their boat, was just too much to bear. They decided to see if they could use their own weight to right the craft. After several tries, they succeeded in getting the boat back on an upright keel. They scrambled in, then used their hands and wet clothing to bale most of the water out. The oars were lost and the sail was either torn away or damaged. The teens were cold, wet and desperate as they huddled together, drifting before the night wind. George said Frank was so chilled he thought he might lose consciousness. He said he kept slapping Frank's face and making him jump up and down to keep alert.

Sometime in the night, a sailing ship passed about thirty feet away. The boys said they yelled at the top of their lungs, but the ship did not stop. Rescue mercifully came at daybreak. A scow, on its way to Windsor, saw the teens and picked them up.

Burning of the *Dalhousie*

On Lake Ontario
Thursday, September 26

A fire broke out aboard the propeller *Dalhousie* in the afternoon, the day after after the ship left Montreal on what was to have been a long trip to Chicago with a load of pig iron and general merchandise. Capt. Maurice McGrath lead an all-out campaign to extinguish the fire after flames were discovered in an aft bulkhead. Someone thought the fire started from a spark from the furnace room. After two hours it was apparent that the ship would be lost.

The steamer came to a stop in the middle of Lake Ontario, about forty-five miles from Niagara Falls. There the crew prepared to launch life boats. Before they got away the propeller *City of Concord* came alongside and renewed the fight to save the *Dalhousie*. As sailors from the *Concord* turned hoses on the flames, the crew of the *Dalhousie* used the time to save some of their own personal belongings. They dashed below and rescued their clothes, the ship's books and anything else of value that they could still reach. A rope was passed around the burning ship and the *Concord* took it in tow toward the south shore of Lake Ontario. The fire eventually opened the *Dalhousie's* hull and the ship sank about two miles off shore, near the mouth of the Genesee River. The tow rope parted as the ship began to go down. The *Dalhousie* was a mass of flame when it sank in eight fathoms of water. As it slid into the water the fires were extinguished with a loud hiss. Great columns of steam spewed off into the sky overhead.

The crew, including Captain McGroth, mate John Leonard, purser J. M. Morris, and engineer Thomas Hickey, were later transferred to the steamer *Mary Ward*, which took them to Port Dalhousie.

September Death Gale

When the final count was taken, statistics showed that the series of gales that swept the lakes between September 24 and 29 were the most destructive of the shipping season. The wind whipped the lakes for five consecutive days, and from all accounts, as the gales came almost in succession of one another, they seemed to increase in strength and power. Lulls tempted captains to think the storm was over and they took their boats back out open water, only to get caught in yet another part of this strange, on-going storm. Sailors said the worst of the blow occurred on Saturday and Sunday, although a lot of boats were sunk on Lake Huron, just off Tawas Point, on Thursday and Friday. When it was over, the *Detroit Free Press* said five propellers, one tug, two barks, one brig, forty-seven schooners, eighteen scows, and nineteen barges were sunk, wrecked, stranded or damaged. An estimated sixty-one sailors from seventeen different vessels died.

The storm was probably no more severe than gales that sweep the lakes on a regular basis. In 1872, it caught smaller wooden-hulled sailing ships, many of them leaky old relics that were commissioned in the post-Civil War years to fill a critical need for ships, especially for the lumber business. Many of the lost boats were from strings of lumber barges that could not prevail against the storm. Not all of the wrecks are accounted for in this record. Their stories could not be found.

Wreck of the *Galena*

Thunder Bay's North Point
On Lake Huron
Tuesday, September 24

Captain Warren Broadbridge spent Tuesday afternoon supervising the loading of two hundred and seventy-two thousand feet of lumber. He also had a wary eye on the sky while his ship, the propeller *Galena,* lay moored at Alpena, Michigan. Even when he brought the ship into port earlier in the day, the weather was windy and boisterous. By late in the afternoon, it was clear that a gale from the southwest was building. Broadbridge knew his scheduled trip to Chicago was going to be rough. He was still considering the weather as passengers began boarding the ship that evening. Departure time was 11:00 PM so the five passengers booked for the trip didn't start arriving until after supper. He made the decision by 10:00 PM to sail on time, in spite of the storm. He told first officer William Walker that he knew the gale would give him trouble until he cleared North Point, but after that, the *Galena* would have the wind at its stern during the trip north to the Straits of Mackinac.

The captain's concerns about North Point were well founded. The *Galena* steamed out of the safety of Alpena harbor promptly at 11:00 PM. Broadbridge said he steered in what he thought was a wider than normal arch around the point and believed he was safely clear of it when he gave the order to turn north. Broadbridge didn't have the benefit of modern radar. The wind blew the boat farther off course than he believed possible. By midnight the ship was hard aground on the outer reef, about a mile and one-half from shore. The ship hit with a jolt that threw passengers from their bunks and rattled pans in the galley. Broadbridge ordered the engines reversed. His first hope was that the hull wasn't damaged and that there was a chance to get free. The steamer didn't budge. Inspection revealed a large hole in the hull near the bow. The seas were pounding the *Galena* with such force, he stopped trying to get free, and instead ordered the hull scuttled. This was done to stabilize the ship and try to keep it from pounding to pieces. Wooden ships didn't take much of an assault from heavy seas, while stranded in a bed of rocks. Since the *Galena* was in shallow water, it sank only a few feet before settling with a slight list. The cargo of heavy lumber creaked and groaned as it adjusted to the odd tilt of the ship.

Thus began a period of anxious waiting for the estimated twenty souls on the steamer. The storm continued throughout that night and the following day. With the engine room flooded there was no heat. Waves continually rolled over the decks, buffeting the cabins and threatening to destroy the ship. The steamer *Wenona* passed the wreck on Wednesday morning, cautiously making its way against the gale as it

*The bark **Erastus Corning** anchored in a gale off Lake Huron's Thunder Bay and offered to rescue the crew of the wrecked steamer **Galena**. Institute for Great Lakes Research.*

entered Thunder Bay after slipping down the coast from Mackinaw City. The captain said the crew and passengers were still aboard the wreck, large waves were breaking over the upper decks and cabins, and he was afraid the steamer would break up. He said he could not get close enough to take survivors for fear of his own ship ending up on the reef with the *Galena*. At about 2:00 PM the barque *Erastus Corning*, under the command of Captain George H. Clarke, spotted the *Galena* while passing the point on its way down the lake to Detroit. Clarke ordered the *Corning's* anchors dropped about two miles off the point, and he sent four sailors in a yawl boat to attempt a rescue.

The sailors reached the *Galena* after an hour of hard pulling. They were surprised to find the people aboard the wreck in relatively good spirits and the crew still hopeful that the storm would abate so the ship could be saved. Nobody was willing to leave the *Galena* and take advantage of the *Corning's* offer of rescue. By nine o'clock that night, however, Broadbridge was having second thoughts. The storm did not ease at sundown, as he had hoped. If anything, it was showing signs of getting worse. He decided that if four sailors from the *Corning* could successfully bring a yawl across two miles of that violent lake to check out his crew's well-being, he could get a yawl across the one and one-half mile stretch of open water to shore. A boat was lowered from its davits on the lee side of the wreck, and a delegation consisting of Captain Broadbridge, clerk J. C. Gilchrist, second officer M. Cook, engineer E. Moshier, a wheelsman, a watchman and all five passengers, made the perilous journey to shore. First officer Walker and a small number of crew members elected to stay with the ship. Broadbridge's boat arrived on shore about an hour later. Everybody was cold and very wet. They walked several miles to Alpena, arriving early Thursday morning.

By Thursday afternoon, the *Galena* was showing signs of breaking up and Broadbridge abandoned his command. He brought a boat back to the *Galena* and took off the rest of the crew. Several trips apparently were made, because the sailors also started removing personal things, including tools, bedding, and even some of the ship's furniture. A story in the *Detroit Daily Post* said one of the boat's arches was gone, and it looked as if the hull was broken. The storm that wrecked the *Galena* didn't quit for several more days.

Wreck of the *Iron City*

In Lake Erie
Off Sturgeon Point
Wednesday, September 25

It was hard for Capt. George Bennett, master of the tug *M. I. Mills*, to keep his composure after Capt. Richard C. Gunning turned up alive to tell his side of the story. Gunning accused Bennett of running off and leaving his barge, the *Iron City*, and the crew to perish after a line between the two vessels broke during the storm off Point Albino, Ontario. "The tow line parted about 7:30 PM," Gunning said. "I called to the *Mills* to take a new line I threw from the barge but he refused. I then asked him to take off my crew, but the *Mills* steamed off."

Bennett had a different story. He said the gale overtook the two vessels while they were on route from Cleveland to Buffalo with a load of over thirty-one hundred barrels of oil. He said the gale was so bad that when the line parted, it was impossible to get a new one attached. Neither vessel was equipped with a yawl boat to help carry the line across. As night closed in, Bennett said he decided to run the *Mills* to Buffalo and then go out the next day and try again. He believed the barge could drop anchor and safely ride out the storm. When the *Mills* steamed back the next day, Bennett said he found the *Iron City* abandoned and in a wrecked condition about two miles off Sturgeon Point. The barge was tipped on one side, the stern under water, and the anchor was dragging in forty feet of water. The deck was separated from the hull and barrels of oil were floating around in that part of the lake. Bennett assumed that Gunning and his crew of four men and one woman were drowned.

Gunning said the *Iron City* was listing and in trouble even before the *Mills* left it. "I called the crew to the deck and we threw a quantity of the oil overboard. Everybody put on life preservers and then got on the hurricane deck. When the boat went over (capsized), I fell in the water and I didn't see the crew again." Gunning said he went in the water about 9:30 PM. He said he found a plank and held onto it for the rest of the night and until noon the next day when he was picked up by the schooner *Red White and Blue.*

About the same time that Gunning fell from the ship, the rest of the crew was floating off on the hurricane deck as it broke loose from the barge. Everybody hung on and waited to be rescued. Sailor John Ryan said the raft floated close to Point Albino, but then the wind shifted and it blew in a southwesterly direction back across Lake Erie. He said the *Mills* passed them twice the next morning as it searched for the wrecked barge, but they were not seen. They came ashore, still alive and clinging to the wreckage, later in the day.

Tugs recovered most of the cargo of oil. The barrels were floating all over the lake. The *Iron City* was formerly a propeller by that same name that plied for many years on Lake Superior. It was built at Cleveland in 1856. It was not a large ship, measuring only six hundred and seven tons.

Aboard the *Phil Sheridan*

On Lake Huron
Off Pointe aux Barques, Michigan
Friday, September 27

There was a lull in the storm so the propeller *Phil Sheridan* left Bay City with a cargo of wooden barrels and shingles. The *Sheridan* cleared Saginaw Bay, and was somewhere off Point aux Barques when the gale rekindled with new life. Captain Van Patten turned the boat around with thoughts of running back to the safety of the Saginaw River. As the *Sheridan* turned, it broached to and nearly foundered. The seas washed away the deck load, stove in gangways and forward bulwarks. Mountain high waves washed over the pilot house, throwing fear into the hearts of the wheelsman and other officers who thought they might be swept overboard. The *Sheridan* battled the gale all night and part of the next day before it finally got back to Bay City. Van Patten said it was the worst storm he could remember in his forty years on the lakes. The fuel ran so low the crew burned part of the cargo just to keep the ship going. The vessel was severely damaged when it steamed back into port at about 8:30 PM Saturday night. It was still afloat and the crew was glad to be alive.

Wreck of the *John H. Drake*

Off Lincoln Park, Illinois
On Lake Michigan
Saturday, September 28

The gale caught the propeller *New Era* and two tow barges, the *John H. Drake* and *City of Erie* in the southern end of Lake Michigan on Saturday night. The master of the *New Era* headed for Chicago, hoping to get to safe shelter before the night was over. The steamer made it, but the two barges were left on the lake to fend for themselves when the tow line parted sometime around midnight.

The *Drake* turned abreast of the seas and, as the crew struggled to save the ship, a giant wave swept Captain Mulvany and the ship's mascot, a large Newfoundland dog, overboard. They perished. The *Drake* drifted ashore about two miles north of Lincoln Park. The sailors lashed themselves to the rat lines and hung there, facing the storm and taking a lashing from both wind and waves, until dawn. The tug *Tom Brown* found them and brought them ashore. The sailors were so exhausted and suffering from exposure they could hardly walk. The storm continued for yet another day. The next night, the *Drake* broke up and was declared a total wreck.

The *City of Erie* came through the storm in much better shape. The crew dropped anchor and rode out the storm. By Sunday morning, the barge lost part of its deck load. It had a lot of water in its hold and was showing a slight list, but it was still afloat when a tug towed it into the harbor. The crew spent a bad night on the lake, but everybody was all right.

The Strange Case of the *G. J. Whitney*

On the Great Lakes
Somewhere in northern Lake Michigan
Saturday, September 28

When the schooner *G. J. Whitney* turned up missing, the people who watched it sail from Chicago on Friday, September 27, were haunted by the strange events of that afternoon. They said the ship was displaying flags at half mast, a traditional symbol of mourning. Also, the American ensign was flying upside down, with the union down. It was almost as if Capt. Wellington Carpenter and the nine members of his crew knew they were sailing off to their deaths in one of the worst storms of the season.

The *Whitney* left Chicago with nearly twenty-four thousand bushels of corn in its holds, bound for Buffalo. It is generally believed the ship foundered somewhere in northern Lake Michigan when the worst of the gale struck. No one ever saw a trace of this ship or any of the crew again.

The schooner seemed to have been hexed for about a year before it disappeared. It was wrecked on Sugar Island late in the fall of 1871, on a trip from Buffalo to Chicago, then was raised and repaired in the spring of 1872. On its first trip of the year, the *Whitney* got driven aground at Vermillion, Ohio. It was refloated and towed to Detroit for repair. It was on the very next trip that the *Whitney* was lost with all hands. The crew included Captain Carpenter; his brother, Lafayette Carpenter, the ship's mate; and the cook, Kate Elliott.

The *Corsair* Saga

On Lake Huron
Off Sturgeon Point
Saturday, September 28

Their names were Thomas D. Foley and Morris Rady, both from Oswego, New York. Their story of survival at sea, following the sinking of the ore laden schooner *Corsair,* was classic. They lived for thirty-six terrible hours, clinging in storm-tossed waters to the wreckage of the *Corsair's* cabin, before they were rescued by the steamer *City of Boston.*

The *Corsair,* under the command of Capt. G. H. Snow, was caught by the gale in the middle of Lake Huron. The ship was pounded by both wind and sea for hours before it started leaking at about 10:00 PM. After the leak was discovered, Snow set a new course for Tawas which made the schooner ride easier in the seas. He also put his crew to work doing everything possible to keep the ship afloat until land was reached. Foley and Rady told of Herculean tasks. They said the men threw part of a fifty-ton deck load of iron ore overboard and took turns manning the hand-operated pump. Even with the new course, the seas rolled across the *Corsair's* decks and the men said they were often standing knee deep in water. The wind shifted at 3:00 AM and the heavy seas put additional stress on the ship. After this, they said the wind seemed to blow with more power than ever. Snow gave up trying to reach Tawas and tried to turn the ship into the wind. His new plan was to drop anchor and ride out the storm. There was so much water in the hold the *Corsair* would not obey its rudder. The ship broached and became caught in the trough of the seas. The ship soon became sunk to its deck and everybody knew that the end was near.

Foley and Rady told of general confusion and terror during the minutes before the *Corsair* sank. As the waves rolled over them, they said the ship's cook, Elizabeth Kelso, wife of seaman James Kelso, started screaming. Captain Snow delayed giving the order to abandon ship until it was too late. When Snow finally ordered the yawl lowered from the davits, Rady said one of the blocks stuck, and he jumped into the boat to cut the ropes with his knife. At that moment, the *Corsair* gave a lurch, the cargo shifted, and the vessel plunged bow first. As they rode the ship to the depths, both Foley and Rady said the last thing they heard was a loud scream from Mrs. Kelso. They said the scream rang in their ears for about an hour after the ship and all of its occupants were gone. The other members of the *Corsair's* crew to die were Harvey T. Crouch, S. E. Perkins and Philip T. Rowlinson.

Rady said he grabbed the yawl and went down for a while with the *Corsair*. He said he sank deeper and deeper until he finally let go of the wreck and rose back to the surface. Minutes later he was surprised to find that the yawl was floating in the water with him. He realized that it also broke away from the ship at about the time he let go. Someone called his name and he found Foley sitting in the boat. Foley said he didn't know how he got there. He remembered being swept from the ship as it sank, and then being turned over and over before he found himself inside a partly submerged lifeboat. The yawl was shattered on one side, and was in such a poor condition, the men felt that they probably couldn't survive the storm in it. About thirty minutes later, just as dawn was breaking, they spotted a portion of the quarter deck and a cabin roof floating a few feet away. The wreckage formed a raft of about ten feet square. The two decided they had a better chance on that, so they abandoned their broken yawl and climbed on.

The two men, already exhausted from the battle to keep their ship afloat, now found themselves clinging to a small piece of wreckage that would be their home for another thirty-six hours. One can not imagine the dispair they felt, clinging

*This rare picture is believed to show the bow of the **City of Boston**. The ship rescued two survivors from the sunken schooner **Corsair**. Institute for Great Lakes Research.*

to that makeshift raft. They said they remembered seeing Mrs. Kelso's body float past, and entertained thoughts of how the woman was still around to haunt them. By noon the first day, they were so chilled they said they found it difficult to speak to one another

Two ships passed, but they did not come close enough for anybody on their decks to hear the shouting by Foley or Rady, or see their small forms in the water. Then, at about 3:00 PM, a steamer appeared. It was going to pass close by, and the two men thought that at last, they would be rescued. They shouted and waved, and then grabbed one another in joy as the ship turned toward them. The storm was still raging, and as the ship slowed, it turned in the trough of the seas and nearly capsized. To save his command, the captain ordered the engines ahead at full steam. The vessel steamed away, leaving the two men to their fate. If they knew the boat, Foley and Rady were kind enough not to name it. They said they both weeped like children after that.

No more ships were seen that day, and the men realized that they were going to spend another night on the raft. By then they were so tired, cold and hungry that the thought was almost impossible to accept. They talked a lot about death. They spent the night giving messages to one another to pass on to friends and family. Foley said he came to a point where he wanted to die. He said he talked about just letting go. Rady crawled up to him and struck him with his fist, challenging him to hang on a while longer. Morning came. By then the storm was somewhat abated, and the men could ride their raft without clinging so hard. They marveled that they still lived. Ships passed in the distance, but, again, there was no rescue. The day got longer, and they feared that still another night awaited them. At 3:30 PM, the *City of Boston* approached. By 4:00 PM the steamer was close enough that the men on its decks could hear the shouts of the two men in the water. The ship stopped and Foley and Rady were rescued, alive!

Collision in the Storm

On Lake Huron
Somewhere off Tawas, Michigan
Saturday, September 28

A string of seven ore-laden barges got separated in the storm from the towing steamer *John Prindiville*. During the confusion, the schooners *White Squall* and *Libbie Nau* accidentally bumped into each other. The collision put a hole in the side of the *White Squall* and it sank, forcing the crew of eight, under the command of Capt. David J. Stimson, to cast off in an open boat. It was a long, three-hour pull against an angry sea, but at last land was in sight. The men began to believe they would survive. Luck wasn't with them, however. The boat capsized in the surf, throwing seven of the sailors out to drown. Only seaman Frank Root survived. Root was lashed to the boat and was still there when the craft washed up on the beach a few minutes later. The life boat was designed to automatically turn itself upright again. Drowned were Captain Stimson, mate John Trawlson who was Stimson's father-in-law, and sailors William Nelson, Harry Miller, G. Scabranch, William Sawsman and a Swede known only as John.

One other barge from the string got in trouble that day. The *Southwest* blew aground in Tawas Bay. The crew scuttled the vessel to keep it from breaking up, then went ashore in a lifeboat. The *Prindiville* was bringing the string of vessels from Lake Superior to ports on Lake Erie when the storm hit.

Wreck of the *York State*

On Lake Michigan
At Milwaukee Harbor
Saturday, September 28

The wrecking tug *Leviathan* was at work salvaging the grounded schooner *York State* on South Manitou Island when the storm came. The *Leviathan* took the schooner in tow and the two ships were doing a good job of battling the gale as they approached the safety of Milwaukee harbor. As they got close to the breakwater, the hawser broke and the schooner fell off into the seas, broached, then was driven stern first into the rocks alongside the pilings of the old government pier. The next morning, people on shore saw a signal of distress flying in the schooner's halyards. The crew was clinging to the rigging, trying to escape the seas that were sweeping the decks. The government revenue cutter *Andrew Jackson* sent a lifeboat and safely removed all eight members of the crew.

Blown Backwards

On Lake Huron
Off Port Hope, Michigan
Saturday, September 28

The tug *Vulcan* was caught by the gale on Lake Huron with a lumber raft in tow from Bay City, bound for Tonawanda. The wind howled unencumbered across the open lake from the northeast, whipping up colossal seas. In spite of its powerful engines, the tug was driven backwards toward the rocky Michigan coast. To fight the storm, the *Vulcan* had both anchors down and its engines running full speed. Both the tug and its log raft were dragging closer and closer to destruction, however.

To save the ship, Capt. M. McGregor ordered the raft cut loose. The tug now could hold its own against the gale,

STEAMBOATS IN ICE

but the wind blew the raft into the rocks, where it broke up. Heavy logs tumbled ashore at Port Hope and the immediate area. Some of them caused extensive damage to private property, including the village dock.

Slamming into Logs

On Lake Erie
Near the Mouth of the Detroit River
Saturday, September 28

The steamer *Jay Cooke* was carrying a number of excursionists on what was supposed to have been a pleasure cruise across Lake Erie from Put-In-Bay to Detroit. The storm wrecked the pleasure part. The passengers were anxious and many were suffering from seasickness as the *Cooke* rolled in mountain high seas.

Capt. L. B. Goldsmith brought the *Cooke* skillfully through the gale and by 2:00 AM he was confident that the worst was over as the vessel approached the mouth of the Detroit River. Suddenly there was a loud snapping sound and

*The steamer **Jay Cooke** was damaged when it ran into a drifting log raft at the mouth of the Detroit River. Institute for Great Lakes Research.*

the ship lurched. There was a ringing of alarm bells and the steamer's massive side-mounted paddle wheels cranked to an abrupt stop. Passengers and crew members rushed out on the soggy decks, anxious to learn what terrible calamity had befallen the ship. The *Cooke* was adrift in the middle of a sea of logs, apparently from a raft that broke away from a towing barge. Nobody saw the danger until one of the logs got wedged in a ship's wheel.

Inspection showed that the wheel was damaged. The engineer reported, however, that once the log was removed the wheel could be repaired so that the steamer could continue on its way. The problem was that the ship could neither go forward nor backward without striking more logs and doing more damage to the paddles. Goldsmith's decision was to do let the steamer stand in place until daylight. By morning the wind blew the *Jay Cook* and the logs aground on the Canadian shore, about a mile below Amherstburg. The passengers were removed in a yawl and taken to Amherstburg.

Surviving the Storm

On Lake Erie
Off Rondeau, Ontario
Saturday, September 28

The schooner *American Champion* was caught in the tempest on Lake Erie and things were not going well. The ship was laden with lumber from Michigan forests and the weight of the cargo, including a large deck load, put the vessel at risk as the seas attacked from across the starboard bow.

When the ship started taking on water, Capt. R. H. White steered for shelter off Rondeau Point. He brought his nearly waterlogged vessel as close to shore as he dared and dropped anchor, hoping to ride out the storm. Then the wind shifted to the west and the anchor began to drag. The *American Champion* was in danger of going aground. As the ship flooded and sank lower and lower in the violent seas, the crew scrambled into the rat lines and hung there. They watched as the waves tore away the lumber lashed to the deck. White encouraged everybody to hang on. The next day the storm subsided and the men launched the ship's yawl boat and rowed to shore. A tug later pulled the schooner to Buffalo.

The ship was in a bad condition when it arrived. Portions of the cargo were torn away. The stern of the *American Champion* was twisted and splintered. The crew kept the ship together by roping the stern to the main mast.

Lost Lumber Barges, Part One

On Lake Huron
Off Port Hope, Michigan
Saturday, September 28

The steamer *Colin Campbell* lost a string of six lumber laden barges early in the morning off Port Hope. The barges were the *Isabel, Plymouth, Ritchie, Waurecan, Colorado* and *Emerald*. All were carrying crews of about six or seven people each.

The *Isabel* hoisted sail and let the wind blow it on a natural course west to Port Austin, Michigan, on Saginaw Bay. While making the trip, the ship took a fierce beating and the deck load of lumber started to shift. Capt. John Burton and two other volunteers went on the deck to try to save the cargo. While they were on the lumber pile, the ship was struck by a giant wave that carried some of the load overboard. Burton and the two sailors went with it. The sailors got pulled back on board the *Isabel* by the others, but Burton was lost. His last words were: "Oh, my God . . ."

The *Isabel* and *Plymouth* got to Port Austin and anchored there. The *Ritchie* and *Waurecan* went to Tawas and the *Colorado* was reported safe at Tawas Point. Nobody heard from the *Emerald* for several days and it was feared lost. Then it was found ashore near Port Hope. The crew was alive and well. The barge was recovered intact with its cargo.

Lost Lumber Barges, Part Two

On Lake Erie
Somewhere off Port Burwell
Sunday, September 29

The tug *William A. Moore* and its tow of lumber barges *Ajax, Adriatic, Joseph* and *Baltic* were making their way up the lakes empty from Buffalo to Saginaw when the final stage of the storm hit them early Sunday morning. The wind whipped around to the southwest and swept the lake with such power that the *Moore* was quickly in trouble. The crew cut the tow barges loose to save the *Moore*. The *Joseph, Adriatic* and *Baltic* hoisted sail and started for Long Point, hoping to find shelter. The next day, only the *Joseph* was found anchored at the point. The *Adriatic* and *Baltic* were missing.

Captain McKee, master of the *Joseph* said he saw the *Baltic* founder. McKee told a strange story of watching the crew launch a lifeboat and start rowing for the *Joseph*. When they were part of the way, the boat turned around as if the sailors were trying to return to their sinking ship. Before they completed the turn the lifeboat capsized and the crew of six men and one woman were lost. One unidentified sailor, who claimed to have been aboard the *Baltic,* was taken off a small offshore island a few weeks later. This man had a different story to tell. He said he rode a plank to the island and last saw the other members of the crew floating away on the ship's hatches. The *Baltic's* master was Capt. John Van Norman of Bay City, Michigan. The *Baltic* had a colorful history. The ship was a steamer when launched at Buffalo in 1847. It was converted for use as a lumber barge in 1865.

The *Adriatic*, under command of Capt. David Murdock also of Bay City, took four other men and two women to the bottom of Lake Erie with it. Nobody saw it sink. The barge just disappeared in the gale. The cook was Julia Halliday.

The *Ajax* was not equipped with sails so all the crew could do was drop anchor and ride out the storm. That worked. The barge survived and was picked up by the *Moore* the next day.

Lost Lumber Barges, Part Three

On Lake Huron
Off Tawas Bay
Sunday, September 29

The lumber laden barges *Table Rock* and *Ontario* were in a string of vessels under tow behind the tug *Zouave* when the storm struck them off Tawas Point. The bitter wind whipped the lake to a frenzy and the old wooden hulled barges took a pounding. Waves swept the decks, carrying away deck cargo and drenching the crews. The *Table Rock* and *Ontario* both waterlogged and broke away from the tug. The vessels were on their own in a storm that was sinking ships around them without reservation. The *Ontario* survived the storm. It was found the next day half sunk, but anchored off Fish Point, about seven miles north of Tawas.

It was a different story for the *Table Rock*. As the vessel drifted before the wind and sea, it began falling apart. Capt. James McAuley knew his crew was in serious trouble. Then out of the storm steamed the propeller *Sandusky*. When they saw the drifting schooner the *Sandusky's* crew tried to help. They were not successful. The *Sandusky* almost capsized when it tried to pull alongside the half submerged barge. Rather than take a chance of losing his ship and the people aboard the *Sandusky,* the captain elected to continue north to Alpena and let the crew of the *Table Rock* attend to their own fate.

The barge drifted ashore on Tawas Point where it pounded to pieces. All crew members except one man, who lashed himself to the yawl and drifted ashore in it, died. McAuley, the mate and the mate's wife were last seen floating away on the ship's cabin.

The *Sandusky* later anchored successfully in Alpena harbor, even as heavy seas were rolling over both harbor piers. The captain said the gale was among the worst he had ever been in. To get to port, he said he had to keep a full head of steam up in the boilers.

*This artist's picture shows how the steamer **Detroit** looked when it had paddle wheels and was busy carrying passengers and freight across Lake Michigan. Institute for Great Lakes Research.*

Lumber Hookers Aground

On Saginaw Bay
Lake Huron
Sunday, September 29

The gale was in its final fury. The propeller *Detroit,* a massive old ship that had seen better times, was struggling against the storm with the barge *Hunter* in tow. The two ships had loaded with lumber at Saginaw, and were starting on a trip to Chicago. The storm refused to let the *Detroit* out of the bay. The ship steamed hard against the wind for hours but made no headway. The old wooden hull strained against the storm and the ship shuddered each time the seas slammed their way across the bow. Water seeped into the hold and adjoining engine room. After a while the leaks got worse and the water got deep enough to put out the ship's fires.

Both vessels became drifting wrecks. They washed on the rocks above Harrisville, Michigan, west of Port Austin, about a mile apart and forty rods from the beach. The crews struggled for survival. The mate of the *Detroit* later said it was the worst storm he had ever been in. He said the sea came at them like mountains and the wind lifted huge sheets of water that dropped down over everybody, drenching them constantly. The woman cook on the *Hunter* died from exposure. The rest of the crew members got ashore the next day on rafts.

The tugs *Rescue* and *Kate Moffatt,* from the Coast Wrecking Company, arrived the next week to begin salvage operations. Pontoons were attached and both hulls were released the week of October 14. Only the *Hunter* was saved. While they were towing it into deep water, two chains parted and the *Detroit's* hull cracked and sank. The ship was declared a total wreck. The *Detroit* originally was launched at Buffalo in 1859 as a side-wheeler. In its day the vessel was considered one of the finest passenger boats on the Great Lakes. The *Detroit* and a sister ship, *Milwaukee,* shared a regular route between Grand Haven, Michigan, and Milwaukee, Wisconsin.

The *Montezuma*

On Lake Erie
Off Port Stanley
Sunday, September 29

The brig *Montezuma*, under the command of Capt. Francis Mcavoy, wrecked near Port Stanley, along the north shore of Lake Erie. Because there were no survivors, nobody knew just what happened.

This was known: The *Montezuma's* entire crew, including Captain Mcavoy and his wife, were lost. The crew members were last seen floating away from the wreck on the top of the cabin, which separated from the hull. The cabin later floated ashore, but no bodies, alive or dead, were found with it. Mrs. Mcavoy's body later washed ashore. She had a money purse containing one thousand, four hundred dollars, strapped to her. The *Montezuma* was carrying one hundred and twenty-five thousand feet of lumber. The ship was built in 1847 so was twenty-five years old when it wrecked.

STEAMBOATS IN ICE

*The superstitious sailors on the **Lake Michigan** threw a coffin containing the body of a passenger's relative overboard when the vessel got caught in a bad storm on Lake Michigan. Institute for Great Lakes Research.*

The Unwanted Corpse

Somewhere on Lake Michigan
Sunday, September 29

After the storm, the Canadian steamer *Lake Michigan* was found drifting without power by the propeller *Lac La Belle*. A tug was called to pull the *Lake Michigan* to safety. Crew members told a strange story about traveling through the storm with a corpse, which they believed was bringing the ship bad luck.

Although pictured in this book as a steam barge, the *Lake Michigan* was designed in 1872 to carry both passengers and freight. There was a Canadian family on board for this trip, traveling to Illinois. Their cargo included the remains of an ancestor who died twenty-seven years earlier. They actually had the casket and it's morbid contents dug up for the trip. Plans were to rebury it when they arrived at their new home. This information was known to the ship's superstitious crew.

As the storm intensified, the sailors grew uneasy. Every man blamed the coffin stashed away below deck. They began murmuring. They believed that their situation, aboard a wooden ship in a severe storm at sea, was caused by the presence of that body. Some of the men were sure they would never reach port unless something was done. When the engine failed and the ship became a drifting, helpless wreck the crew revolted. In spite of pleadings from the captain and the family, the sailors threw the coffin and its mouldering remains overboard.

Strangely enough, the *Lake Michigan's* luck changed just after that. The *Lac La Belle* found the vessel in its broken down state, the storm abated, and finally a tug arrived to pull the ship to safety. The sailors were convinced they did the right thing.

Other Gale Casualties

Many other boats were sunk or damaged by the September gale. Their brief stories are as follows:

Lake Huron

❱ The schooner *Neshoto*, carrying iron ore, foundered off Sturgeon Point early Sunday. Capt. B. Gray and his crew started for shore in the ship's yawl but only Gray and the mate made it. Reports said either four or five sailors drowned. One man, possibly the mate, suffered a broken leg. The ship sank in forty feet of water and the masts and sails could be seen from shore the next day. People said they also saw what appeared to be a man hanging on the rigging.

❱ The schooner *Minnie Mueller*, with a cargo of pig iron, disappeared on route from Frankfort to Detroit. The ship left Frankfort, on Lake Michigan, on September 20 and never arrived at its destination. The *Mueller* was presumed sunk in Lake Huron with all hands.

❱ The propeller *Benton* was driven aground Sunday while docked at Tawas to load shingles. The ship's line parted. After the storm ended, the *Benton* worked its way back into the lake under its own power and continued on to Detroit. The vessel was leaking, but the pumps kept it afloat until it reached dry dock.

▶ The bark *Jesse Hoyt,* loaded with grain, lost its main topmast and was nearly wrecked in Tawas Bay.

▶ The barge *Sweepstakes,* in tow behind the steamer *Jenness*, took heavy storm damage by the time it arrived at Port Huron. The cabins were demolished, the deck and bulwarks were stove in, part of the deck load of lumber was swept away, and the ship was waterlogged.

▶ The barge *A. Lincoln* went ashore one mile below Au Sable. The crew was saved but suffered from exposure.

▶ The schooner *Eagle Wing*, Captain Banner, almost capsized when its cargo shifted. The crew threw ten tons of ore off the deck before the ship got back on even keel again.

▶ The barge *Globe*, loaded with lumber, dragged its anchor at Tawas Point, then drifted on the rocks where it took a severe pounding.

▶ The schooner *Rebecca* blew ashore at Alabaster dock near Tawas City. The ship was carrying a load of plaster.

▶ The schooner *Narragausett* was carrying ore when it blew ashore in Hammond's Bay at the Straits of Mackinac. The schooner later was refloated. The *Naragausett* was making its first voyage on the lakes after returning from several years of ocean service.

▶ The dock and warehouse at Forester, Michigan, were destroyed. The warehouse contained ten thousand bushels of wheat waiting to be shipped.

Lake Erie

▶ The barks *William Howe* and *Prince of Wales* went ashore below Port Dalhousie. The vessels were both in tow of the propeller *Argyle.*

▶ The bark *Butcher Boy,* carrying a partial load of coal, was one of several vessels anchored to wait out the storm at Bar Point, at the western end of Lake Erie. The *Butcher Boy's* anchors dragged and the ship was driven into the side of the schooner *Annie Vought.* The force of the storm caused the two ships to slam into each other repeatedly until they were both extensively damaged. The destruction ended when the *Butcher Boy* sank.

▶ The steamer *Atlantic* was caught by the gale while

traveling from Cleveland to Detroit with passengers and freight. The ship arrived in Detroit on Sunday morning with extensive damage. The passengers were frightened and seasick. They said one wave smashed a gangway so the ship's decks were constantly deluged until the crew made emergency repairs. At another heart-stopping moment the ship nearly capsized.

▶ The schooner *Colonel Hathaway* arrived in Detroit after spending a fearful night off Marblehead. The crew threw a deck load of coal overboard to save the ship.

▶ The barge *William Treat* was driven aground at Bar Point. The vessel later was pulled off and towed to Detroit.

▶ The scow *Agnes*, laden with staves, went ashore near Rond Eau, Ontario.

▶ The schooner *R. J. Gibbs* was driven ashore at Port Stanley, Ontario. The ship was loaded with railroad iron, on its way from Buffalo, New York, to Toledo, Ohio. The tug *Hector* pulled the *Gibbs* free.

▶ The schooner *Yankee Blade* went aground on the east side of Point au Pellee. The ship was carrying one hundred tons of pig iron from Kingston to Chicago. The *Blade* also was pulled free.

Lake Michigan

▶ The steamer *Equinox* went aground on South Manitou Island. The Steamer *City of Fremont* pulled it free. There was extensive damage. The seas smashed the *Equinox's* gangways and the captain and mate were hurt. The crew jettisoned part of the cargo, trying to get the ship afloat.

▶ The bark *Cecilia* also went ashore on South Manitou Island.

▶ The schooner *Mary Nau* foundered at Death's Door off Green Bay. The ship, under the command of Capt. S. Gunderson, was carrying fifteen hundred barrels of salt from Detroit, bound for Green Bay.

▶ The schooner *H. A. Richmond* stranded at Cross Village off Grand Traverse Bay. The ship was pulled free by the tug *Leviathan*.

▶ The propeller *Fountain City* broke a rudder off Point Betsey and broached. The ship stayed in that condition for

*The schooner **Butcher Boy** sank in a collision on Lake Erie during the autumn gale of 1872. Institute for Great Lakes Research.*

more than four hours, in danger of capsizing, before repairs were finished. The *Fountain City* finally wore around and continued on to its destination at Pine River.

▶ The schooner *C. C. Butts* shipped water. It arrived at Racine in a waterlogged condition.

▶ The schooner *Jenny Lind,* loaded with wood for Chicago, arrived in Milwaukee in a waterlogged condition. A large portion of the ship's deck load was gone, the main gaff was broken and the main sail split.

▶ The schooner *Hattie Johnston* went ashore on Old Mackinac Point on Friday night. It was pulled off by the propeller *Nashua* and towed to Milwaukee. The *Johnston's* foremast was sprung, and the main boom, cross trees and gaff were gone.

▶ The scow *Cherubusco* was driven ashore at Death's Door bluffs on Green Bay.

▶ The bark *James. C. King* and the bark *Lydia Case* were both blown ashore at Spider Island Reef, off Green Bay.

▶ The schooner *Mary Booth* went aground on Pilot Island, at Green Bay.

▶ The schooner *D. R. Martin* waterlogged at South Manitou Island. It was carrying lumber.

▶ The schooner *Colonel Heg* was driven ashore at Manistee, Michigan.

▶ The scow *Neil Cochrane* was loaded with lumber when it blew ashore near Elm Creek.

Lake Ontario

▶ The schooner *Alpha* of Hamilton, Ontario, went ashore four miles east of Oswego. The ship was carrying a cargo of lumber from Toronto to Oswego.

▶ The scow *Ada* grounded between piers at Port Washington, Ontario.

▶ The schooner *Annie Belle Chambers,* laden with lumber, capsized in the bay near Toronto. The crew clung to the wreck until rescued by local fishermen.

Lake Superior

▶ The schooner *Maple Leaf* went ashore on Isle Royal. The crew of five was taken off by the schooner *Hornet.* The wreck was towed to Silver Islet a week later by the tug *Silver Spray*. The seas tore away the ship's foremast, sails, rigging and swept away its cabin.

▶ The schooners *E. C. Roberts* and *A. H. Moss* were scuttled at Marquette to prevent their destruction by the storm.

Wreck of the *B. R. Lummis*

In Grand Traverse Bay
Lake Michigan
Saturday, October 5

The schooner *B. R. Lummis* took a big gash in the side when it collided with the steamer *City of Fremont* Saturday night. The *Lummis* was taking on water. The crew of the *Fremont* tried to tow the stricken ship to Traverse City before it sank. While on route Captain Starkweather, master of the steamer, ordered the line cast off. He later said he didn't like the way the schooner was pulling and wanted to establish a new one directly from the bow. As soon as the hawser was dropped, however, the lights of the *Lummis* disappeared and the *Fremont* didn't see the schooner again. The *Fremont* steamed off to the nearest port and reported the loss of the *Lummis* with all hands.

Capt. J. W. Jones and his crew weren't finished. All but one man came ashore alive two days later, clinging to the wreckage of their overturned ship after it drifted on the beach near the Traverse Light. Hugh Hazlett of Milwaukee, died from exposure. Jones said the *Lummis* capsized the moment the tow line was dropped, which accounted for the ship's lights blinking out. The crew hung on the wreck until it drifted on the reef. A storm developed and the next day high seas lifted the wreck over the reef and delivered it on the beach. The seas were running so high that the sailors were forced to hang on for a second night before they came ashore.

Bill Angell's Big Mistake

On the Saginaw River
Bay City, Michigan
Thursday, October 10

Bill Angell had an important job as wheelsman on the *Hattie T. Brown*, a steamer ferry that whisked people daily across the busy Saginaw River. Bill never quite lived down his blunder the morning he made a wrong turn into the path of the downbound tug *James T. Ransom*, which had a barge in tow. The ferry was struck broadside. The crash capsized and sank the *Brown* at 10:00 AM. The *Brown*, under the command of Capt. Ans Titsell, was carrying about four passengers; two men and two women. The engineer and two of the male passengers saw that the accident was about to happen. They jumped to the deck of the tug while the two boats were locked briefly together. Everybody else ended up in the water. Nobody was hurt or killed. Captain John Kelley, the *Ransom's* skipper, stopped to pick up survivors. So did the steamer *Morning Star* which was nearby. The *Brown* was raised the next day and soon was back in business.

Burning *China*

On Lake Ontario
Sunday, October 14

  The new Canadian propeller *China,* one of at least two vessels on the lakes carrying that name in 1872, was destroyed and sunk by fire on Sunday night. The steamer, under the command of Capt. Francis Paterson, was carrying three hundred tons of pig iron, wheat, and a quantity of general merchandise when it left Kingston, Ontario, bound for the upper lakes. The fire was discovered already raging out of control below deck when the *China* was only fourteen miles from port. The crew fought the fire anyway. Two other steamers saw the smoke and came to help. They pulled alongside and joined the fire fighting effort with their own pumps and fire hoses. The fire had gained so much headway that the battle was lost. The steamer burned until it sank in shallow water near Snake Island Light. The *China* had been launched at Kingston in April, 1872, and was destroyed only fourteen miles from that spot six months later.

Wreck of the *Lac La Belle*

On Lake Michigan
Off Racine, Wis.
Monday, Oct. 14

  Ed Carney, first mate aboard the Engleman Line steamship *Lac La Belle* was clearly worried when he woke Capt. W. H. Thompson. "Captain, we've got troubles," Carney announced. "The boat's leaking and the pumps can't keep her free. It looks bad." Thompson glanced at his pocket watch as he hurriedly dressed in the dim light of Carney's lamp. It was 12:15 AM. Monday morning. The steamer left Milwaukee, Wisconsin, bound for Grand Haven, Michigan at 9:30 PM Sunday, and Thompson guessed it had traveled about thirty miles. A gale was blowing and the ship was taking seas off the port stern.

STEAMBOATS IN ICE

*Eight persons died when the propeller **Lac La Belle** foundered in a storm on Lake Michigan. Courtesy Milwaukee Public Library.*

Even though he had been awakened from a sound sleep, Thompson's mind was already racing. He sent Carney back to the bridge with orders to turn the ship around for a race back to Milwaukee. He knew it would take more than three hours to make the trip against the wind so he wanted no time wasted. Thompson desperately wanted to know the source of the problem and do whatever possible to save his command. He woke Chief Engineer L. Bennsil and the two men went below to learn what they could. They never found the source of the leak. As they worked their way into the bowels of the ship, the two were stopped by a wave of water breaking through a forward bulkhead. They retreated to the engine room.

"I then went and looked in the fire hold and found the water was ten inches over the floor, rapidly increasing and gaining on the pumps," he later recalled. Thompson then knew that the ship was doomed. After returning to the deck, he told Ned Dowe, company agent who was among the passengers, that "we have got to lose this boat." Knowing this did not stop the captain from putting up a fight. He did all he could to save the *Lac La Belle* and the fifty-two other people on its decks. He sounded a general alarm, ordered everybody out of bed and asked the male passengers to help throw cargo overboard to lighten the ship. The steam pumps were run-

129

ning at full blast and Thompson assigned crew members to also operate hand operated bilge pumps. Down in the fire hold the black gang dipped water with buckets in a gallant effort to keep the fires burning as long as possible.

The rising water soon covered the coal bunkers, and the wet coal began cooling the fires. The ship was losing the steam power it needed to keep both the pumps operating and and the engines running. "We found some barrels of pork and lard in the cargo. I ordered the heads knocked in and the contents thrown in the furnace to get an increase of steam," Thompson said. After that, crew members began breaking up furniture and tearing the ship apart for dry wood to burn. Everyone worked frantically, only to have their hopes of reaching shore shattered at about 4:00 AM when the water rose over the dead lights, and one of them collapsed under the pressure. Thompson said the water now poured into the ship with such force it could not be stopped. "We tried to plug it (the broken window) by stuffing blankets and quilts into it and nailing on boards, but had no success. The water was now up to the bottom grates (of the engine room fires) and the firemen gave up. They said the vessel must sink."

Sometime between 4:00 and 5:00 AM the fires went out, the steam pumps stopped working, and the ship became a sinking, drifting wreck. Sailors continued to operate the hand pumps, buying minutes before the *Lac La Belle* sank. Thompson said he gave the order to abandon ship when he saw that the main deck was about level with the lake. When the order came to launch the life boats, Dowe told of an ugly incident amidships with some of the engine room crew. "The first boat, intended for ladies and other passengers, was taken possession of by an engine greaser, who, armed with a carving knife, kept everybody out but his companion greasers." Rather than fight the men, Dowe said he let them have the boat, but talked them into taking some of the passengers. They agreed and the boat was launched.

Five boats were put in the water, and almost everybody got away on them before the steamer sank. Dowe said Thompson had to be forced to get in the last boat. The captain was trying to pursuade the last handful of passengers to leave the sinking ship with him. "They seemed panic stricken. We used force and succeeded in getting some of the women and children into the boats, but we could not move the men." Dowe, who helped direct the launching of the boats, said they could not persuade five or six men that they must leave the ship or perish. "There were about half a dozen persons on board the sinking steamer who refused to trust themselves in small boats. One of these was S. Wiener (a Milwaukee businessman). He was last seen on the promenade deck in the bow of the boat. Another was the second cook (Henry Sparks), who stood in the forward gangway. There were also one or two persons on the promenade deck. I saw nothing of them after the steamer sank."

An unnamed survivor described Captain Thompson's actions as heroic. He told the *Milwaukee Sentinel* on October 10 that Thompson nearly gave his own life to save the final number of passengers. He said the last boat, a small metal craft was launched, but stood by the side of the wreck waiting as Thompson tried to talk the last hold-outs to get in it with him. "At this time the ship's main deck was a foot under water, and was sinking very rapidly. Mr. Bernard hailed the captain and told him if he wanted to be saved to get immediately into the boat as the ship would sink in a moment. Captain Thompson was up on the promenade deck and got down in the launch by a rope. And with the greatest difficulty the little boat shoved from the side of the sinking ship. We had got barely ten feet when the beautiful propeller went to the bottom."

The story teller said Bernard, the chief engineer, yelled to the men to get from the main deck up on the promenade deck. Bernard was an experienced sailor and knew the wooden upper superstructure would probably break away and float off when the ship sank, giving the men a temporary raft. "They did so as the ship was going down and three men were seen to jump overboard." he said. Bernard said he saw four men in the water, one of them clinging to a timber. "They must have been lost because we couldn't give any assistance without danger of swamping our boat," he said.

"The *Lac La Belle* went down stern forward a few minutes after we left," Dowe said. "She appeared to break in two near the pipes, throwing the engine out, and lifting the cabin into the air with such force as to shatter it into kindling wood. The last object we saw of the wreck was the figure of the Goddess of Liberty, with a small national ensign in her hand, which was mounted on the pilothouse. The figure was floating in an erect position with the flag fluttering in the wind."

The life boats all came safely ashore, or were picked up by passing boats by midday. One man was pulled from the water after clinging to a board for several hours. News of the disaster reached shore with the life boats. The first boat with eleven survivors came ashore at Racine, Wisconsin. The people on that boat included the ship's clerk William Sanderson, Peter Wetter, Mr. Warner and his wife, Robert Fogg, Louis Oerhster, and the ship's chambermaid Rebecca Campbell. Later in the day a second boat came ashore near Racine, and the captain's metal boat arrived near Kenosha. The schooner *Floretta* picked up a boat load of people off Waukegan and the last boat arrived safely at Calumet, Illinois the next morning.

The dead were identified in various newspaper accounts. In addition to Wiener and Sparks, they included H. Freeman, N. W. Gilbert, P. Wyent, R. H. Lippincott, W. Smith Dunning, and one unnamed deck hand. In all, eight persons died.

The steamer was a wooden ship, built in 1864. It was not the newest or fanciest boat plying the Great Lakes in 1872, but it was a faithful visitor between Milwaukee and Grand Haven. It was a large ship for the time, measuring two hundred and seventeen feet from stem to stern. Some said it was popular with passengers who enjoyed the convenience of a regular passage between the two cities. In addition to the twenty-one passengers, the ship was carrying about five hundred tons of freight which included ten thousand eight hundred bushels of barley, a quantity of flour and pork, and boxes of sundry items marked for delivery at Grand Haven stores.

Murder at the Welland Canal

Aboard the schooner *White Oak*
On the Welland Canal
Monday, October 14

Troubles developed among men living in the close confinements of shipboard. When things got out of hand, sailors sometimes used knives or guns to settle their differences. It was a hard way of life somewhat comparable to our American portrait of the old west during the early years.

An argument developed between Captain Coote, master of the schooner *White Oak*, and one of his employees, a sailor identified as John Graham. Nobody knows how long the hard feelings festered between the two men. The *White Oak* was on a long haul, from Chicago to Kingston, Ontario, with a load of grain. The men had been locked together on the slow-moving vessel for days and probably weeks.

Things came to a head while the ship was locking through the Welland Canal, on its way to Lake Ontario and the last leg of the journey. Loud, heated voices were heard. Then Coote drew a gun and shot Graham. The sailor died about an hour later on the main deck where he fell. A coroner's inquest was held at Welland and Captain Coot was jailed on a charge of manslaughter.

Alaska on the Rocks

On the Detroit River
Thursday, Oct. 17

The iron steamer *Alaska* was one of the new "heavyweights" among the lakers. Built the year before at Buffalo for the Anchor Line, the ship measured two hundred and twelve feet and grossed over twelve hundred tons. It was a competitor in the big freight haul between Chicago and Buffalo. The *Alaska* was plowing its way down the lakes with its holds laden with twenty-six thousand bushels of corn, twenty thousand bushels of wheat and eight thousand bushels of

STEAMBOATS IN ICE

*The steamer **Alaska** went aground in Lime Kiln Crossing on the Detroit River. Photo shows the vessel converted as a lumber barge in 1911. Institute for Great Lakes Research.*

barley, bound from the Chicago grain terminals to Buffalo, when it went aground at the notorious Lime Kiln Crossing.

The Lime Kilns, just up the river from Amherstburg, Ontario, were well known to veteran sailors. It was a major trouble spot for ships working their way through the Detroit and St. Clair Rivers between Lakes Erie and Huron. Low water levels in 1872 made the problem even worse. Before the shallows were deepened by the U.S. Army Corps of Engineers in 1874, sailors used to say the best depth any ship could hope for was thirteen feet, and that depended on which way the wind was blowing. Thus it was that the newer and bigger vessels like the *Alaska* often scraped bottom when easing their way down the river with a heavy load.

The *Alaska* got too far off the normal course and hit the shallow rock bottom square on. The ship hit so hard the hull opened and the hold flooded. The grain turned to mush. The damage was extensive. The solution was to hoist steam powered pumps to the deck and get them running full blast. Lighters pulled along side, and a small army of men shoveled the heavy, wet and ruined grain out of the *Alaska's* hold. After enough cargo was removed the ship was refloated on October 21, four days after it hit. It was towed up river, the noisy steam pumps still spewing great streams of dirty water over the sides, until it reached the Detroit dry dock. The *Alaska's* luck improved after that. It remained on the lakes as a freight hauler until 1911, when a Tonawanda lumber dealer converted the ship for use as a lumber carrier. It was changed again to work as a fuel lighter in 1912, and then reduced to be a barge for Canadian owners in 1936. The hull was scrapped at Hamilton, Ontario in 1947.

Blown to Atoms

On Lake Ontario
At Otsego Harbor
Friday, October 25

An explosion ripped the tug *P. P. Pratt* into fragments of junk late in the night. Otsego residents considered it a miracle that there were no casualties. A story in the *Oswego Palladium* described the condition of the *Pratt* as "blown to atoms." Pieces of the ship landed all over the town, but nobody was even scratched. A large piece of boiler, weighing about five hundred pounds, landed at the corner of West First and Cayuga Streets. A piece of the ship's rail was found impaled in the roof of a local church. The stories didn't explain how the explosion happened, or why nobody got hurt on the *Pratt*.

Where is the *Eliza Williams*?

On Lake Erie
Off Rond Eau, Ontario
Tuesday, October 28

The new tugboat *Eliza Williams* was started on its way up the lakes from the shipyard at Buffalo, New York, to a berth at Duluth, Minnesota when something went wrong with the engine. The schooner *Amoskeag* found the vessel adrift early Tuesday morning off Long Point. The winds were favorable, so the *Amoskeag* took the *Williams* in tow on a route toward the Detroit River. Even with the wind at the stern, the task of pulling a heavy tug proved too much for the schooner. The captain of the *Amoskeag* hoped to turn the job over to a steamer as soon as one appeared on the horizon..

The two vessels made their way slowly across the lake all that day but no other ships were seen. That night a gale developed, the wind shifted, and the *Amoskeag* was forced to cut the *Williams* loose off Rond Eau. The *Williams* was last seen drifting off into the night.

Days past and the *Eliza Williams* was not heard from. The ship's owners at Duluth began sending queries about the tug on November 8. Nobody had any information. It was as if the *Williams* had disappeared without a trace. Then, on November 11, the *Williams* arrived at Detroit under its own steam. Captain Greenfield explained that the ship drifted all night in the storm. A tug found it the next morning and towed it into Rond Eau. It moored there until the engine was fixed.

The Ice Returns

November 1 - December 10

STEAMBOATS IN ICE

The Mate and How Many?

On Lake Michigan
Off Sleeping Bear Point, Wisconsin
Wednesday, November 6

The wreck of the schooner *Jennie and Annie* on the Wisconsin coast was commonly reported by the coastal newspapers. As was their custom, the papers copied the story, sometimes word-for-word, from one another. For this reason, the stories were all very similar except for one peculiar point ... there was a difference in the number of people that the newspapers reported killed.

The *Jennie and Annie* was under the command of Capt. S. Prince and carrying twenty-one thousand and five hundred bushels of corn from Chicago to Buffalo when it got caught in a gale at the north end of the lake. The schooner began taking on water. The crew manned the pumps while Prince tried to bring the vessel to shelter. As the schooner battled for survival, the gale tore away the canvas piece-by-piece, until there was nothing left but bare poles. Without sails, the *Jennie and Annie* was unmanageable. The vessel drifted ashore near Eagle Bluffs, directly across the lake from Manitou Island.

As the gale pounded the ship, the stories said the mate and a number of sailors from the crew of ten attempted to swim for shore and were drowned. The *Detroit Daily Post* said two crew members joined the mate and that seven others remained behind to be rescued. The *Detroit Tribune* said the mate and five others jumped overboard to perish. The *Milwaukee Sentinel* said the mate and three crew members drowned.

The other members of the crew stayed with the wreck for forty-eight hours until rescuers on shore could safely launch a small boat and get them off. The schooner broke up after that.

Drifting Sailors

Somewhere on Lake Michigan
Aboard the schooner *Hamilton*
Wednesday, November 6

The leak developed in rough weather and it looked like the schooner *Hamilton* would sink. Capt. Harvey L. Burch had his men working at the bilge pump all day but the water gained. By 3:00 PM, the vessel was waterlogged and no longer answering its helm. The yawl was launched and the crew, consisting of Burch, mate G. H. Hughes, steward Samuel Martin, and sailors D. G. Holcomb, Thomas Williams, Richard Jones and William Backus, left the ship.

The weather was so rough the men remained under the lee side of the sinking schooner until midnight, when the *Hamilton* rolled on its side. The ship didn't sink because it was loaded with lumber. Once it capsized, however, the hull no longer offered shelter. It was a long, cold night at sea for the seven sailors. The gale blew at them from the northwest so they knew their boat was drifting toward the Michigan shore. They huddled together, taking each drenching wave, and waiting for dawn. Someone brought a loaf of bread so they had something to eat.

Land was in sight when the sun came up, and everybody was glad about that. The yawl drifted ashore about 10:00 AM Thursday about a mile north of South Haven, Michigan. The sailors stepped ashore that morning, somewhat cold and weary, but alive. The *Hamilton* was bound from Muskegon, Michigan, to Chicago.

Saving the *Cleveland*

Somewhere on Lake Huron
Wednesday, November 6

The schooner *H. G. Cleveland*, with Captain Vader, was in trouble after a cargo of wheat shifted during a storm on Lake Huron. The problem got so bad that water was sweeping the decks, and the holds were flooding. To save the ship from capsizing, the crew cut away the halyards. As the storm progressed, the seas swept everything from the decks, including the lifeboat and some of the sails and rigging. The crew worked at the pumps, and struggled to keep the ship afloat, but things looked bad. Then came rescue. A tug found the *Cleveland* adrift off Point aux Barques, Michigan, and towed it to Detroit.

Sinking of the *Forest Queen*

On Lake Erie
Off Point Albino, Ontario
Thursday, November 7

It was once a proud steamer hauling passengers and freight, but by 1872 the *Forest Queen* was stripped of its superstructure and machinery and reduced to the role of a worn out lumber barge. The ship was making regular trips behind the steam barge *Burlington* between Bay City, Michigan, and Buffalo, New York. Serving aboard lumber barges was a dangerous job because they were mostly old boats, long past their prime. The *Forest Queen* took its entire crew to the bottom of Lake Erie when it sank in a November gale.

The *Forest Queen* was the last barge in a line of three lumber laden vessels bound for Buffalo when the strain from a storm broke the tow line linking all three barges to the *Burlington*. For a while the barges, identified as the *Kentucky, Star of the North,* and *Forest Queen,* remained tied together. All three boats raised sail and started for shelter together. The *Forest Queen* got separated when the hawser connecting it to the next ship in the line also parted.

Nobody knows what happened after that. The *Forest Queen* disappeared in the darkness. The crew of the *Kentucky* said at one time they passed a man clinging to a piece of wreckage and calling for help. Since their own barge was waterlogged and out of control, they couldn't turn around and pick him up. Killed were Capt. William Walker of Detroit; the mate, William Steva; the cook, Ufary Rose; and sailors J. A. Straub and Alfred Oldfield.

*Early photograph shows the high arches and paddle wheels on the **Forest Queen** when it was a proud freight and passenger hauler. The ship had been stripped down to be a lumber barge when it sank on Lake Erie in 1872.*

The next day the tug *Gardner* searched for the barges. It found the *Star-of-the-North* and *Kentucky* anchored in the bay outside of the Buffalo breakwater. The *Kentucky* was partly submerged, the seas were washing over its decks, and the crew was hanging in the rigging, waiting for rescue. There was no trace of the *Forest Queen.* Captain Walker's body was found December 2, incased in ice, on a beach near Stoney Creek.

The Boston Fire

Boston, Massachusetts
Friday, November 8

The great fire that consumed Boston on November 8, 1872, had an impact on Great Lakes shipping. Historians say this fire, which came on the heels of the Chicago fire in 1871, helped trigger a downturn in business that almost paralyzed the nation's business by the end of 1873. Things got so bad that some ships never got out of port in 1874.

The fire was, in many ways, comparable with the Chicago disaster. It's origins, however, were not as obscure. This blaze started in the furnace room of a four-story wholesale dry goods store on the corner of Summer and Livingston

Streets. The fire raced up an elevator shaft to the top floor, quickly consumed that building, and spread to adjoining four-story buildings. The buildings in that section of the city all had Mansard roofs, providing tall, vacant lofts that created an artificial draft which helped feed the flames. Before long, an entire block was consumed and the conflagration was spreading out-of-control. The flames were so hot they jumped from rooftop to rooftop throughout the city's business district.

Author Robert S. Holzman in his book *The Romance of Firefighting*, said the firefighting effort was hampered by a spread of distemper among the city's fire horses, so that the department had only six healthy animals to drag the heavy steam powered pumpers to the fire. Some equipment had to be pushed around by sheer manpower. In addition to that, Holzman said the fire was burning in the heart of Boston's shopping district where winding, narrow streets made deployment of fire equipment difficult. The water supply was poor.

One eyewitness report published in the *Detroit Tribune* on November 11 said: "The fire was constantly in the air and one building after another caught on the roof....the flames skipped lightly along from one window to another." The fancy granite fronts of the buildings collapsed as the structures burned, making streets impassable and driving fire fighting efforts back. The heat was so intense fire fighters could not get close without having a constant spray of water turned on themselves. "The firemen erected barricades and worked from behind them. But the barricades were burned almost as soon as they were erected," the story said.

The fire created a wind draft as the flames drew oxygen. The wind was so strong some people described it as a hurricane. The wind whipped fire and burning coals into the air. Every building became superheated before it broke into flames like tinder. "The tenement houses at the upper end of Federal Street were now being licked up by the flames, and women, crazed and fainting, were rushing to and fro carrying children, crocks, bedding, and clocks..."

When it was over, nine hundred and thirty businesses and factories and many homes were destroyed. About sixty acres were burned. Losses were estimated at more than one hundred million dollars.

Wreck of the *Willis*

On Lake Erie
Off Point au Pelee
Monday, November 11

    The record of the schooner *Willis* is short. The ship was destroyed in a collision on one of its first trips after coming down the ways at Manitowoc, Wisconsin. The *Willis* was a three masted schooner that measured slightly more than one hundred thirty-one feet in length. It was downbound with seventeen thousand bushels of barley, possibly from Racine, Wisconsin, when it was nearly cut in two by the schooner *Elizabeth Jones*. The collision happened just before daylight and fifteen miles off the Canadian coast. The *Willis* sank in about ten minutes in sixty feet of water. The crew just had time to lower the lifeboat. Everybody was picked up by the *Jones*. The captains blamed each other for not having their lights properly displayed.

Ship Full of Peas

On Lake Ontario
Off Oswego, New York
Tuesday, November 12

    The schooner *William John* sprung a leak while sailing from Trenton to Oswego with thirty-two hundred bushels of peas stuffed in the hold. The crew took turns working the pumps, trying to keep the ship afloat while Captain Savage used all of his skill to bring the aged vessel to port before it sank out from under him.
    It was a race that the crew could not win. The creaking hull seemed to open even wider as the afternoon wore on, and the wind just wouldn't push the ship along fast enough to beat the clock. By 4:00 PM the hull was sunk enough so that the seas were washing across the decks. Savage knew the race was lost. The schooner *Centurion* was passing and saw

that the *John* was going down. It pulled alongside in time to take off the crew. The schooner sank about three miles from Oswego.

Wild Times at Duluth

Duluth Harbor
Wednesday, November 13

A savage winter storm raked Duluth harbor with such strength that it damaged the breakwater then ravaged the boats moored inside. Needless to say, the storm took its toll on vessels caught in the open waters of Lake Superior.

The first casualties were the schooners *Francis Palms* and *Sweetheart,* traveling together with cargos of coal for delivery at Duluth. Both captains were making their first trip on Lake Superior and they hired a pilot to take them across the lake and into Duluth harbor. The pilot miscalculated his position in the storm and missed the harbor entrance. The two boats tried to anchor outside the breakwater but the storm drove them ashore. During the confusion, the mate of the *Sweetheart* fell overboard and for a moment was feared lost. A large wave miraculously tossed him back against the side of his ship where he was grabbed by two of his friends and pulled on board. The crew of the *Palms* got ashore the next day with the help of a breeches buoy attached to a yard arm.

That night the storm got so bad it started tearing away sections of the breakwater. Three vessels moored behind that part of the wall, the steamer *St. Paul,* the tug *Bob Anderson* and schooner *Alice Craig*, were in immediate danger. All three vessels cast off for new locations. The *Craig* fared the worst of the three. It drifted on the rocks and was severely damaged. The tug steamed across the bay to safer quarters. The *St. Paul* got its wheel tangled in the line of another vessel and stranded on the beach with the others.

The Storm at Marquette

On Lake Superior
At Marquette, Michigan
Wednesday, November 13

    The gale from the northeast hit Marquette harbor with the same kind of fury it delivered at Duluth. Ships reeled under the force of it. Here are three stories:
    The propeller *Atlantic* had a narrow escape from the storm as it approached Marquette. The giant waves, forty-five-mile-per-hour winds and heavy snow pounded the boat until windows were smashed and the superstructure began ripping apart. The crew and passengers spent a night of terror hanging onto anything bolted to the deck. For a while most of the people on the steamer had given up all hope of survival. Everybody put on life preservers and prepared for the worst. Many people were praying. Just after dawn the entrance to Marquette harbor came into sight and the ship arrived safely at 8:00 AM. Prayers were answered.
    The steamer *Mineral Rock* was in Marquette harbor, but the gale came with such force the ship dragged its anchors and for a while the vessel threatened to drift on the rocks. Captain West said it was a fearsome gale. The storm was so violent that sections of the Marquette breakwater collapsed from the driving force of the seas. West said his crew attached a hawser from the ship to the pier, which saved the *Mineral Rock* from destruction.
    Capt. C. Peterson didn't think he could bring his command, the schooner *Exile*, safely into the harbor, so he dropped anchor off Chocalay River, about six miles south of town. The storm blew hard all night. Sometime early Friday morning, the ship's anchor chain broke. The schooner drifted toward shore and almost certain destruction. A moment before it struck, a large wave carried the *Exile* up and over a sand bar at the mouth of the river. The vessel came to rest in deep, calm water on the river. Peterson was relieved at first because the *Exile* had escaped. Or had it? It took Peterson a moment to understand the depth of what had happened. Mother Nature apparently had a strange sense of humor. The

STEAMBOATS IN ICE

*The propeller **Atlantic** was nearly lost in a November gale on Lake Superior. Institute for Great Lakes Research.*

ship was appropriately named. The storm had, indeed, exiled the schooner from any more business on the lakes this season. It took a dredge to dig it free the following spring.

Burning of the *John Stewart*

On Lake Huron
Off Sebewaing, Michigan
Sunday, November 17

The little steamer *John Stewart,* owned and operated by Capt. John Stewart, had been aground off Sebewaing for several days. On Sunday afternoon, the boat mysteriously caught fire and burned to total destruction while people on shore watched helplessly.

Stewart and the engineer were among the watchers. They said they didn't know what started the fire. They came ashore a few hours earlier and left only a few coals burning in the cabin stove. They said there had been no other fires going. Stewart suggested arson, but it was never proven. The *Stewart* made regular trips between Sebewaing and Bay City, Michigan.

147

Wreck of the *New Hampshire*

Somewhere on lower Lake Michigan
Monday, November 18

The schooner *New Hampshire* was struck broadside by the schooner *Maggie Thompson*. The early morning crash happened about thirty miles from Chicago, on the lower end of Lake Michigan. The *New Hampshire's* crew knew their ship was lost. The collision crushed the hull below the water line and it was sinking fast. Capt. Charles Peterson and the seven other members of his crew abandoned ship, each man scrambling to the deck of the *Thompson* even before the *Thompson* pulled away. The *New Hampshire* sank minutes later.

Sinking of the *Minot Mitchell*

On Lake Michigan
Near South Manitou Island
Monday, November 25

The schooner *Minot Mitchell,* Captain Tierkoff at the helm, was laden with cut grindstones from the quarry at Grindstone City, Michigan. The *Mitchell* was sailing across Lake Michigan, bound for Chicago, when it sprang a leak in a storm.
The crew went to work on the bilge pumps. At first they seemed to be keeping ahead of the water and Tierkoff thought the *Mitchell* would weather the storm. By noon, when about six miles off the Manitou Islands, the storm intensified. As the seas pounded the wooden ship, the leak got worse and the water gained on the pump. The storm also ripped the ship's canvass sails. By late in the day the *Mitchell* was a sinking ship drifting out of control.
The crew escaped in the life boat minutes before the *Mitchell* sank bow first in about thirty fathoms of water. The crew was picked up by the propeller *Chicago* about two hours later.

STEAMBOATS IN ICE

*The Canadian steamer **Mary Ward** was destroyed after it grounded on Georgian Bay. Eight people died. Institute for Great Lakes Research.*

Wreck of the *Mary Ward*

On Georgian Bay
Near Collingwood, Ontario
Monday, November 25

It was a calm, clear night when the coastal steamer *Mary Ward* hit the shoal off Collingwood and crunched to a sudden stop. The pilot mistook a shore light for the Collingwood signal light and took a wrong course. While the accident was an inconvenience for the passengers and crew, Captain William Johnson wasn't worried. The ship wasn't damaged and the lake was so calm he felt that there was no immediate danger. He sent crew members Frank Moberly and A. M. Corbett to shore in a small boat to notify authorities and make arrangements for the passengers to be removed the next morning. Johnson's unconcern was a mistake. Winter was dropping down over the lakes that night with great speed and fury. A raging storm was sweeping down from the northwest. It was a storm packed with subzero degree temperatures, heavy snow and high winds. Before it was over, many a good ship including the *Mary Ward* and eight souls on her decks would be lost. The change in the weather would be so dramatic that the lakes would be frozen shut by the time this gale blew itself out.

One unidentified man who spent the night aboard the steamer said he thought the passengers should have been put ashore immediately. He said he felt a terrible sense of foreboding as he stood on the deck, listening to the laughter of the crew and passengers while watching heavy, black and swiftly moving clouds build overhead. He said his alarm grew when the wind shifted, the stars disappeared, and he heard an ominous moaning sound in the ship's rigging. "I suggested to the watchman that a storm was brewing and that he contact the captain. This he did and the captain recognized the danger at once and began blowing the *Mary Ward's* whistle and calling all the hands on deck."

By the time Captain Johnson took action, it already was too late. The storm developed quickly. By dawn the souls on the *Mary Ward* were greeted with blowing snow and a biting cold wind. Powerful breakers were rolling over the ship's stern. "In a few hours we were all hanging on for dear life and most of us had become reconciled to our fate," the man said.

John Stephens of Owen Sound, one of the ship's owners, was on board. Stephens wanted to take a life boat to shore. Crew members Richard Reardon and William Rorke pitched in to help. Passengers W. H. Coldwell, John W. Taylor, Charles Campbell, Henry F. Chadwick and Robert Blyth all got in the boat with them. Before it got only a few yards the boat capsized and all eight men drowned. The rest of the ship's crew and nine other passengers stayed aboard the *Ward* until that afternoon when fishing boats took them off.

They escaped just in time. By that evening the storm was raging in all of its fury. It blew hard for several days. When it was over, the *Mary Ward* was a pile of rubble. The cabins were torn away and the ship's back was broken. Remnants of the wreck still remain on that reef. The *Ward* was carrying a cargo of salt and coal oil. The ship was bound from Sarnia to Collingwood, and had stopped at Tobermory and Owen Sound on the way.

An Old Relic Burns

At Bay City dock
On the Saginaw River
Wednesday, November 27

While ships and men were facing a killer storm sweeping the lakes, the steamer *George W. Reynolds* was lighting up the night sky at Bay City. A fire of unknown origin destroyed this historic relic and almost killed the engineer, who was sleeping in one of the cabins.

The fire was so spectacular that it brought three different fire departments to the docks between 2:00 AM and 3:00 AM. The fire was threatening the dock and a nearby lumber mill where logs were stacked, waiting for shipment in the spring. To save the mill, fire fighters pushed the burning boat out in the river and then scuttled it. The *Reynolds* was being laid up for the winter when the fire broke out below deck. The *Reynolds*, which made regular trips on the river between Saginaw, Bay City and Pine River, usually wintered at Saginaw. This year the steamer made one trip too many and got caught down river by ice forming up stream.

Jupiter and *Saturn*

On Lake Superior
Near Vermillion Point
Wednesday, November 27

They had the names of planets but the *Jupiter* and *Saturn* were really just ordinary working barges in the business of hauling iron ore. After the storm the names were marred because they sank together taking the lives of fifteen sailors. The tragedy helped bring about the construction of four new government life saving stations on the shores of Lake Superior. The *Jupiter* and *Saturn* were two of several vessels lost in the storm, and their crews were among many sailors who drowned. The fact that they were lost together, and that

STEAMBOATS IN ICE

the crew of the steam barge *John A. Dix,* which had them in tow, lived to tell what happened, helped dramatize the story.

Captain Joseph Waltman, master of the *Dix,* said the three vessels left Marquette, Michigan, at 3:30 PM Tuesday. The *Dix,* a retired government revenue ship, was purchased that season by E. B. Ward of Detroit for use as a tug. The two barges were each laden with about four hundred and sixteen tons of iron ore, bound down the lakes for Wyandotte, Michigan. At first, there was a light breeze blowing from the southeast and Waltman said that even though it was late in November, the weather was pleasant. When a light head wind developed that night, Capt. Peter Howard, master of the *Jupiter,* and Capt. Richard Stringleman, skipper of the *Saturn,* reefed the barge sails because they were no longer helping the *Dix.* The sky was overcast and it had started snowing. Then at 4:00 AM, when the wind veered to the northwest, Waltman said he noticed the barges were under full sail again. He said he felt then that the trip was going so well, and the barges were making such good time, that he thought they would arrive at Sault Ste. Marie within a few hours.

What Waltman didn't know as he entertained those thoughts, was that an ugly winter gale was bearing down on the three ships. It was coming with such speed and force that within twenty minutes, the crews of all three vessels would be in a battle for their lives. He said the storm hit with such power it parted the tow cable to the *Jupiter* almost immedi-

*The **John A. Dix** had the barges **Jupiter** and **Saturn** in tow when the barges were lost with all hands in a November storm on Lake Superior. Institute for Great Lakes Research.*

ately. The *Saturn* broke away and drifted off into the gale by 6:00 AM. The storm front blasted the boats with heavy snow, high winds and fast dropping temperatures. Within hours the thermometers were reading below zero degrees, and at one point the gauges recorded temperatures as low as minus eighteen degrees. Waltman said the *Dix* was in such a fight for its own survival, he could not to turn around and try to save the barges. He said they were both provided with good sails, pumps and life boats, which was the best anyone could hope for under the circumstances. By the time the *Dix* steamed to the lee side of Whitefish Point, the decks were coated with about a foot of ice. The crew used salt to help chip it away before the *Dix* continued on to Sault Ste. Marie.

While under the protection of the point, Waltman said everybody kept an eye out for the *Jupiter* and *Saturn,* hoping they would catch up with the *Dix*. The two schooners never arrived. Later, the steamer *China* reported seeing the masts of the *Saturn* where it sank about three miles above Whitefish Point. The spars of the *Jupiter* were found about twelve miles west of there. Nobody will ever know what the crews of the two vessels endured before they died. The next spring, the bodies of two sailors were found on the beach. It was evident that they reached shore and crawled a few hundred feet out of the water before freezing to death. The area was uninhabited and the men had no chance of finding shelter. Lost among the *Jupiter's* crew were Captain Howard, George Halverson, John Stevens and Peter Perken. Listed among the crew of the *Saturn* were Captain Stringleman, Harvey Swisher, William Langendorf and his wife, James Knight, Archibald Cummings and a man named Wilson.

The *Dix* didn't reach Sault Ste. Marie until the following spring. The ship was one of a fleet of steamers and barges caught in the offshore ice that week. The high winds and sub-zero temperatures brought an abrupt end to the shipping season and caught many vessels still out of port.

Close Call for the *Middlesex*

Somewhere on Lake Superior
Wednesday, November 27

The gale nearly capsized the schooner *Middlesex*. At about 4:00 AM the storm front caught the ship with such force that the vessel went temporarily over on about a forty-five degree angle. The deck cargo broke loose from its ropes and shifted. Captain Davis and his crew hung on for several long moments, expecting the vessel to go completely over. Finally the ship partly righted itself again.

The *Middlesex* was still afloat, but it now had a serious list because of the shifted deck load. Davis put the men to work throwing cargo overboard. It was dangerous work because the storm was howling across the rolling decks and the seas were building. All of this threatened to carry the sailors to their death. As it was, the storm swept away the ship's lifeboat and caused extensive damage to the sails and rigging. The efforts by the crew, however, got the ship righted again.

The schooner made its way into Walska Bay and anchored there, protected from the gale. By then the *Middlesex* had developed a serious leak. The pumps froze so the crew slipped the anchor and ran the boat ashore near Point aux Pine. The schooner sank in shallow water. The crew climbed into the rat lines, there enduring the snow, spray and extreme cold until the tug *W. D. Cushing* rescued them.

Rescue at Erie

On Lake Erie
At Erie, Pennsylvania
Wednesday, November 27

When the schooner *Rio Grande* went ashore while trying to make Erie harbor Wednesday morning, the people on shore started thinking about ways to rescue the crew. The lumber laden schooner was driven on a reef and monster seas could be seen washing over the decks. There was concern that the ship might break up.

Captain Downs, a local tugboat operator, borrowed a yawl from the schooner *Ottawa,* which was docked in the harbor. He enlisted the help of men from the government gunboat *Michigan,* also moored there. Downs brought his tug *Dragon* close to the *Rio Grande,* then, with the help of the sailors from the *Michigan,* he tied a line on the yawl and floated it down wind until it bumped alongside the wreck. In this way the rescuers successfully removed the woman cook. Six other members of the crew decided to go ashore in the *Rio Grande's* life boat. The seas were too high to row out to the *Dragon,* so everybody pulled for the beach and got there safely.

Capt. Ed Collins said he ran the ship into the point after mistaking a light on a hill east of the harbor for the harbor light.

Bad Times for the *Burlington*

Point au Pelee Passage
Lake Erie
Friday, November 29

The wooden propeller *Burlington* was still on the job late in November, even though winter was closing in on the Great Lakes with vengeance. Even before the storm, heavy ice was forming on the lower lakes, and many vessels were laying up. The *Burlington* was a lumber hauler, engaged in pulling barges laden with hardwood and pine from Michigan to ports on Lake Erie. This season already had proven itself disastrous to the *Burlington* and its tows. The ship lost three barges in a Lake Erie gale on November 7, and one of them, the *Forest Queen,* sank with the loss of its crew of seven sailors. Now the *Burlington* was breaking through the ice in Point au Pelee Passage, towing an empty string of lumber barges north to Bay City, Michigan. The steamer's crew was trying to finish one last trip before winter forced the rugged old ship to quit.

*The **Burlington** was sunk by ice on Lake Superior. Institute for Great Lakes Research.*

The storm struck forcefully and without warning. As it battled its way, a large block of ice sliced a hole in the *Burlington's* side, causing the ship to sink quickly in shallow water. The tug *Prindiville* picked up the barges and took them to Amherstburg, on the Detroit River. The *Burlington* was raised and towed to Detroit for repair one week later.

Joyful Survival

On Lake Erie
Off Point au Pelee
Friday, November 29

The schooner *James F. Joy* was hooked to a tow line behind the steam barge *S. C. Sheldon,* on route from Cleveland to Detroit, when the storm caught the two vessels off Point au Pelee. The air got so cold that ice began forming on the hulls and the *Joy* began getting weighted down. When the tow line parted, the *Sheldon* turned around and steamed back to Cleveland, leaving the schooner to carry on against the gale alone.

Things looked bad for a while. The crew of the *Joy* raised sail, but the ship was so laden with ice that it was difficult to steer. Frosted gray seas rolled across the decks coating everything with still more and more of the terrible ice. The sailors suffered from the constant drenching and the intense cold. The main mast cracked and then fell from the weight of ice collecting on the sails and rigging. Late in the afternoon the tug *Balize,* under the command of Capt. James P. Young, steamed by and took the *Joy* in tow to Detroit.

A Man and a Boy

On Lake Erie
Off Cleveland harbor
Thursday, November 28

The *Sunrise* was a schooner-rigged fishing tender owned and operated by Capt. Robert Wilds of Cleveland. On Thursday afternoon, just hours before the storm swept Lake Erie, Wilds set sail from Cleveland, bound for nearby Put-In-Bay, with a load of ten tons of coal, ten barrels of crackers, a barrel of coal oil and a box of cove oysters. The cargo was small for most lake vessels, but just fine for Wilds, who earned extra money making customized coastal trips. Also on board the *Sunrise* was a young unidentified boy, who served as Wilds' entire crew.

Nobody thought about the *Sunrise* for a while after the boat sailed off. Then on Friday morning, as the coast was being buffeted by the storm, people along the river said they saw a capsized boat about two miles from shore, and two people clinging to it. The tug *Scott* built up steam and ventured out in the tempest to take a look, but nothing was found. Later, the *Sunrise* washed ashore near the waterworks inlet pipe and broke up. There was no sign of Wilds or his youthful helper. They perished in the storm.

More Lost Barges

On Lake Erie
At Middle Sister Island
Saturday, November 30

  As the storm swooped down over Lake Erie on Friday, it caught the tug *Torrent* with a string of six coal laden barges in tow, on their way from Cleveland to Detroit. The gale was so violent that the vessels, identified as the schooner *J. W. Sargent* and barges *Morning Star, Ritchie, Ontario, John F. Warner* and *Ottawa*, were soon overpowered by the seas and the heavy ice that was building up on the ship's hulls, decks, masts and sails. Capt. Thomas Hackett, master of the *Torrent*, said the southwest wind was so strong that the boats could not make headway. He tried to reach shelter behind Middle Sister Island, in the heart of a chain of islands at the eastern end of Lake Erie.

  The battle went on most of the night, and the vessels seemed to be gaining against what was by then described as a "perfect hurricane." Capt. R. Wynue, master of the Canadian schooner *Celia Jeffery*, which was anchored under the lee of Middle Sister Island, said he watched the *Torrent's* battle to bring its string of vessels out of the gale. He said the trailing barge, *Ottawa*, foundered at about 9:00 AM. At about the same time, the tow lines to the other vessels parted, releasing all six barges into the gale. Wynue may also have watched the *Ontario* sink. He said he saw a second, unidentified barge go down during a heavy squall about 2:00 PM. "It was impossible to render any assistance because of the heavy wind and the sea." The *Ontario* was never seen again.

  The *Ritchie* was driven ashore on the island. The other three boats successfully anchored behind the island. Even there they had trouble. The storm brought such an extreme drop in temperature that by the next day, ice had formed on the lake and the barges were frozen in place. Neither the *Torrent* nor the wrecking steamer *Magnet* could break them free after that. The crews were taken off and the three barges were left in the ice. The *Sargent* did not survive the winter. When tugs went out the next spring, the schooner was gone. The

*The **Torrent** appears on the job towing barges on the St. Clair River. The tug lost six barges on Lake Erie in 1872. Institute for Great Lakes Research.*

shifting ice apparently crushed the ship's wooden hull and it sank.

Other Casualties

Many other ships were sunk or wrecked in the storm which swept all four of the Great Lakes. Their stories appear as follows:

Lake Erie

▶ The schooner *W. M. Grant,* under command of Capt. O. Donahue of Cleveland, was carrying coal for Chicago when it developed a leak, waterlogged and got driven ashore eight miles south of Point Betsie at 5:30 PM Thursday. The crew spent a night of suffering as the gale swept the decks with snow and freezing spray. The lifeboat was smashed but somehow the sailors escaped to shore the next morning.

▶ The schooner *Kate L. Bruce* went aground on a reef at the head of Lake Erie. The *Bruce* was carrying coal bound from Buffalo to Chicago.

▶ The bark *Board of Trade* went aground somewhere on Lake Erie.

Lake Michigan

▶ The schooner *Edward Kanter*, under the command of Captain Weeks, blew ashore near Leland, Michigan. The ship was carrying railroad iron from Buffalo to Chicago. The crew experienced intense cold and suffering before they escaped. The *Kanter,* which was only a few months old, broke up and became a total loss.

▶ The schooners *Souvenir* and *North Star,* and the scow *Minnie Corlet* were driven ashore near Pentwater, Michigan. The crew of seven was lost from the *Souvenir,* four sailors perished on the *North Star,* and one man died on the *Corlet.* The vessels were owned by a Pentwater firm. They left port together earlier in the day with lumber.

▶ The propeller *J. Bertseky* went ashore near Escanaba, Michigan. The ship was carrying iron ore.

▶ The schooner *Morning Star*, carrying shingles, capsized and drifted ashore near St. Joseph, Michigan. Crew member William Conley drowned.

▶ The schooner *Delaware* stranded near Holland, Michigan. The crew escaped.

Lake Superior

▶ The schooner *William O. Brown*, Capt. Robert Mannifig of Cleveland, Ohio, left Duluth with its holds laden with wheat for a final trip of the season. It disappeared with all hands..

▶ The schooner *Golden Rule* drifted into Walska Bay in a wrecked but still floating condition. Its bulwarks were stove in, the rudder torn away, the sails torn and the rigging extensively damaged. The ship drifted helplessly, an ice-covered derelict, until it blew ashore. The crew suffered from severe cold and many members had their limbs frozen.

▶ The schooner *Marquette* went ashore at Grand Island. The ship was laden with iron ore bound from Marquette to Cleveland.

Lake Huron

❱ The bark *Northwest,* laden with twenty-seven thousand bushels of wheat from Chicago, was driven ashore near Port Hope, Michigan. The ship was pulled free the next day by the tug *Quayle.*

Lake Ontario

❱ The schooner *William Elgin*, laden with wheat from Hamilton, Ontario, bound for Oswego, New York, went ashore about thirty miles west of Oswego.

Sailors On Snowshoes

While the gale played havoc with the smaller sailing ships, most larger vessels survived the storm, but ran into trouble when subzero degree temperatures put an abrupt freeze on Lake Superior and the northern fringes of Lake Huron. A number of ships found themselves locked in the ice at the entrance to the St. Marys River, and they remained trapped there for the winter.

After losing the consorts *Jupiter* and *Saturn* to the storm, the steamer *John A. Dix* arrived at Sault Ste. Marie, only to join a growing fleet of ice-locked vessels. Capt. Joseph Waltman found that he had no choice but to accept that strange winter anchorage. Among the others were the steamers *Japan, Peerless, St. Louis, Arizona, Cuyahoga, Daniel Lewis,* and the bark *Cambridge.* Word came that the steamers *Trusdell, Menominee* and *Norman* were spending the winter frozen in ice on Walska Bay, on Lake Superior, and numerous vessels, including the steamers *St. Paul* and *Atlantic,* and the schooners *Kimball, Farwell* and *Metropolis,* were frozen in on Mud Lake. The steamer *Arctic* was caught in the ice on Portage Lake.

The propeller *St. Paul,* under the command of Captain McIntyre, arrived at the Sault Ste. Marie locks in time to slip through the locks, but then got caught in the deep freeze

STEAMBOATS IN ICE

on shallow Mud Lake, where the water turned to solid ice even as the steamer was working its way through. The unexpected lockup was disappointing for the officers and crew, who were looking forward to ending the season and getting home to spend Christmas with their families. When it was clear that the *St. Paul* was not going to budge again until the spring thaw, the crew decided to strike out on foot across the ice. That decision almost cost the sailors their lives. Three days after the *St. Paul* ground to a stop, a gang of sailors walked to Detour, thirty miles to the south, battling the extreme cold and deep snow. They stayed at Detour for several days until the weather broke, then set off in small boats across the Straits of Mackinac on the next leg of their journey.

On December 7, at about the same time the crew of the *St. Paul* was leaving Detour, the steamer *Benton* was making a late season stop at Cheboygan, Michigan, a few miles across Lake Huron. Some sailors from the schooners *Metropolis, Farwell* and *Kimball* were there, looking for a ride to Detroit. They said their boats were among the fleet locked in the ice and they had just hiked down from Mackinaw. They told how sailors from many different vessels were also walking down that week on snowshoes. C. A. Chamberlain, the owner of the *Benton*, was aboard. He ordered his ship to the straits to search for any sailors still on route. The *Benton* arrived at Detour on Monday, December 9, and learned that the crew of the *St. Paul* left the night before in open boats for a forty mile

*The **St. Paul** was one of several steamers caught in the ice at the close of the 1872 shipping season. Courtesy Institute for Great Lakes Research.*

trip to Mackinaw City. In the meantime, the men of the *St. Paul* were in trouble. After a day on the lake, they seemed to be making little progress and they were in danger of freezing to death. The seas were running high and the cold was causing ice to form on everything. The sailors were nearly perished when the *Benton* found them on Tuesday morning. The *Benton* then fought its way through the building ice fields to Port Huron, and spent the winter there. Lake St. Clair was frozen shut.

A story in the December 24 edition of the *Milwaukee Sentinel* told how large numbers of sailors walked through the woods from Sault Ste. Marie that month on snowshoes, traveling an estimated two hundred miles before finding railroad service at Au Sable. Some hitched rides to Au Sable aboard logging trains operating in the forests further north. The story noted that Sault Ste. Marie was "about as bad a place as can be found on the whole chain of lakes" to be stranded because of its remoteness. The only way out for the sailors was to walk, since there were no railroads operating. Towns were few and far between, and there were no hotel or general accommodations for housing and feeding such a large number of people. Walking out of the wilderness was hazardous because there already was an estimated twenty or more inches of snow on the ground, the weather was severely cold, and it was going to be such a long walk, the men needed to carry a lot of food and camping equipment on their backs. That took planning.

Groups of walkers started out on December 5, 6 and 7 from Sault Ste. Marie. Everybody wore snow shoes, and the first group hired a guide to bring them through the woods. It took the men about two days to traverse the sixty miles to Mackinaw. There a tug took them across the straits, and they walked south to Cheboygan. At that point the men stayed over for about two days, stocked up on supplies, and then continued walking south to Au Sable. The trip took another four days. Listed among the hikers were Capt. Stone of the steam barge *Joseph S. Fay;* Captain Lawless, master of the schooner *Escanaba;* Captain Raynor of the schooner *W. B. Ogden;* Captain Wood of the schooner *William Schupe*; and the master of the schooner *Oak Leaf.*

163

*The steamer **Benton** rescued the crew of the **St. Paul**. Institute for Great Lakes Research.*

Broken Rudder

On Lake Huron
Near Alpena, Michigan
Saturday, December 7

The reason the *Benton* was roaming around in northern Lake Huron so late in the season was that it was on a rescue mission for the propeller *Wenona*. The *Wenona* damaged its rudder off Thunder Bay while on a trip to Cheboygan with supplies.

The *Benton* and tugboat *Sweepstakes* were sent from Detroit to assist. The *Benton's* job was to take off the cargo and bring it on to Cheboygan. This job was successfully completed on December 7, the day word reached Cheboygan that sailors were coming down on foot from Sault Ste. Marie.

The *Sweepstakes* rammed its way through the ice on Lake St. Clair and brought the disabled *Wenona* back to Detroit on the same day. They were among the last boats to get through the ice between Port Huron and Detroit.

Fighting Ice and Snow

On Lake Erie
Off Cleveland, Ohio
Sunday, December 1

The steamers *James Fisk Jr.*, under the command of Captain Moore, and *Canisteo,* Captain Thorn, were trapped in an ice field. The two vessels steamed in convoy from Cleveland harbor the day before. Their masters had thoughts of making one last trip to Chicago before laying their boats up for winter. They struck ice at the dummy light, almost as they were leaving the harbor, then spent several hours pushing, and ramming their way slowly out into Lake Erie. Night fell and the two ships laid over until daylight. On Sunday morning, the captains found their boats surrounded by ice measuring from four to six inches in thickness. They ordered steam up and began the battle all over again. Two hours later they worked their way into open water. By then, however, the *Fisk* was taking on water. The ship had taken a hole in its wooden hull near the stem. To make matters worse, a heavy snow was starting to fall. Moore ordered his crew to work, drawing

*The **James Fisk Jr.** developed a leak while trying to break through the ice at Cleveland. Institute for Great Lakes Research.*

STEAMBOATS IN ICE

one of the ship's canvass sails over the bow and wrapping it around the hull. The canvass slowed the leak enough that the pumps kept ahead of the water in the hold. With this problem solved, Moore next turned the *Fisk* around, and with the *Canisteo* still steaming alongside in escort, the two vessels started back through the ice to Cleveland. The snow was so heavy the sailors lost their bearings. As they made their way south toward land, both steamers blew their whistles, hoping somebody would hear them and offer some kind of help.

Captain Gouler, the Cleveland lighthouse keeper, heard the whistles and guessed correctly what was needed. Gouler first went to the local railroad yard and got someone there to ring a bell on one of the tenders. Next he went aboard the steamer *Java*, which was moored in the harbor, and talked the crew into getting up enough steam to blow its whistle. The noise of both the bell and the whistle guided the lost ships safely into harbor that afternoon.

Back and Forth Across Lake Michigan

Caught in shifting winds
Wednesday, December 4

When the schooner *Home* arrived at Pentwater, Michigan, late Wednesday night, the crew jumped from the ice-caked decks and some sailors may have kissed the ground. They were very glad to be alive. They told an incredible story of being tossed by changing winds on a zigzag course which carried them across Lake Michigan four times before they made port. They were beginning to think they would perish at sea.

The *Home* set sail four days earlier from Manistee, Michigan with a load of lumber for Milwaukee. When it weighed anchor Sunday morning, the schooner took a southwest course with a northeast wind at its stern. When about thirty miles off Sheboygan, the wind shifted and blew a gale from the northwest. The storm stripped the schooner of its deck load and drove it back toward the Michigan coast.

STEAMBOATS IN ICE

The wind shifted again to the east at about 4:00 AM Monday, just as Big Point Sauble was in sight. This time the storm blew the *Home* back to the lee of the light at Manitowoc, Wisconsin. The ship couldn't clear Two Rivers Point. Before the crew could decide what to do, they said the wind shifted once again and began blowing a gale from west northwest. The tired and worn sailors could not believe they were again getting blown east toward the Michigan shore.

All this time, nobody slept and there was hardly time to eat. The men were cold, extremely tired, and fearful they would never set foot on land again. They made the last trip across the lake under high seas that carried away the ship's head lamps and covered the deck, sails and rigging with a deadly coating of ice. The crew gave themselves up for lost. Then at about 9:00 PM Wednesday, the Pere Marquette light was seen. That light gave a final glimmer of hope to a desperate crew. Sometime around midnight, the *Home* slipped into Pentwater harbor.

*The **St. Albans** was one of the steamers trying to make a final trip of the season but got stopped by ice on Lake St. Clair.*

167

One Last Try

On Lake St. Clair
In the Ice field
Monday, December 9

     The Northern Transportation Company tried hard to extend the shipping season for a few more weeks in December. Four company steamers, the *City of Boston,* under command of Capt. John Brown; the *Champlain,* Capt. Ira Bishop; *St. Albans,* Capt. J. J. Knapp; and *Lawrence,* Capt. A. Reed, left Detroit at noon Monday, bound for Chicago with thirteen hundred tons of miscellaneous freight. Their skippers had instructions to break through the ice in Lake St. Clair.
     When they got in the lake, they found the ice was about six inches thick. The *St. Albans'* bow was armed with an iron sheeting, but the iron cracked when the ship attempted to ram its way through. The steamer also lost about forty feet of rail. The *Champlain* developed a serious leak. The four vessels gave up and returned to Detroit.

Summing Up

Other Wrecks of 1872

Numerous other vessels were sunk, extensively damaged and wrecked during the year, but not enough information could be found to offer complete stories:

❯ The schooner *Len Higby* went ashore near Milwaukee, Wisconsin, on Lake Michigan the first week in March. A winter storm hampered salvage work, but the *Higby* later was brought into port.

❯ The schooner *Mail,* loaded with stone from Kingston, Ontario, bound for Toronto, went ashore on Lake Ontario's Fish Point on April 27.

❯ The schooner *Star of the North,* laden with railroad ties, capsized Saturday, May 11 in a sudden squall on Lake Erie, near Point aux Pelee. The crew survived. The Coast Wrecking Company salvaged the schooner a few weeks later.

❯ The tug *H. P. Smith* was destroyed by fire while pulling a barge on the Saginaw River, near Bay City, Michigan on Monday, May 27. The fire was discovered about 9:00 PM. It spread so fast through the wooden ship that the crew just had time to run the vessel to the river bank and jump off.

❯ Another blaze destroyed the tug *Isabella* at Orilla, Ontario, near Toronto, at 3:00 AM Tuesday, September 3. The fire threatened the town's lumber mills so fire fighters pushed it out in the lake and let it burn.

❯ The schooner *St. Andrews* collided with the schooner *M. S. Wilcox* in Lake St. Clair on the night of Thursday, September 26. The *Wilcox,* laden with grain from Chicago, was anchored, possibly waiting out heavy weather. Neither vessel sank, but both boats took extensive damage, especially to the sails, masts and rigging.

❯ The schooner *Mountaineer,* owned by Capt. S. R. Drummond, grounded Thursday, October 10 on Lake Huron while downbound from Marquette with iron ore. The ship broke up in a storm a few days later. A story in the *Huron County News* at Harbor Beach, Michigan, said the wreck happened one mile north of that community.

❯ The schooner *Challenge,* commanded by Captain Woolenow, stranded against the north Muskegon pier on Lake

Michigan during a storm on Saturday, October 12. Before help arrived, the vessel broke up. The crew escaped.

▶ The steam barge *Mary Jarecki,* laden with iron ore from Escanaba, went aground in fog on Summer Island, at the entrance to Green Bay on about October 24. The barge *Fred Kelley,* which was in tow, narrowly missed going on the rocks too. The wrecking tug *Leviathan* pulled the *Jarecki* free.

▶ The schooner *C. C. Griswold,* Capt. J. M. Hand, sailed from Marquette on Wednesday, October 28 with a cargo of iron ore and disappeared. All eight members of the crew perished. The wreck was found the following spring on the Michigan coast between Grand Marais and Two Heart River. Four bodies were found on shore near the wreck by local fishermen.

▶ The barge *Planet,* loaded with lumber, went to pieces during a gale November 7 at Two Rivers, on Lake Michigan. The crew escaped. In earlier years the *Planet* had been a well-known passenger ship on a run between Detroit and Lake Superior ports.

▶ The bark *Cherubusco* was laden with lumber when it waterlogged in a storm on Lake Michigan on about November 16. The captain ran the ship ashore near North Bay to give his crew a chance. Everybody spent hours clinging to the rigging until the tug *Ben Drake* picked them up the next day. The vessel broke up.

A Dangerous Profession

Statisticians recorded two hundred and eleven deaths among sailors during the 1872 shipping season. One hundred eighty-nine of them were from drowning, three were murdered, and the rest died from falls, fires or other causes. As grim as the numbers appear, they reflect a relatively low average for the period. For example, two hundred seventy-two sailors died in 1871. The loss of a single passenger boat with a hundred or more lives would have nearly doubled the number. Not all of the deaths are recorded in this book, although an attempt was made to find them all. Unfortunately, some of the victim's names were lost in the dust of time. The following names are of people killed and seriously hurt. It was compiled from obituary notices and news stories in newspapers published all along the Great Lakes shoreline. They do not include the deaths recorded elsewhere in this book.

▶ Abraham Selligo, a sailor on the schooner *H. Grandy*, was seriously hurt when he fell eighty feet from the rigging to the deck at Detroit on Friday, April 12.

▶ George Williams, cook aboard the propeller *Phil Sheridan,* lost his balance, fell overboard and drowned while drawing a bucket of water in the Detroit River on Monday, April 15. The *Sheridan* was tied up at the Detroit dock at the foot of Second Street when it happened.

▶ Thomas Sexton, crew member aboard the schooner *Jennie and Annie,* drowned Monday, May 6 off Lake Erie's Long Point after falling from a plank he was sitting on. Sexton was hanging over the side of the ship and scraping paint from the hull.

▶ John Fox, a blind passenger, drowned Wednesday, May 8, after he missed his footing boarding the steamer *Rochester* at Mill Point, on Lake Ontario. A crewman saw Fox fall in the water, dove in and pulled him out. Fox was revived after he was rolled face down on a barrel, but he died a few hours later at a nearby hotel.

▶ Capt. John Reed, master of the bark *John Breden*, tumbled overboard and drowned while the ship was moored at Buffalo, New York, early in the morning on Thursday, May 9. Reed was last seen when he came aboard about midnight after a night of heavy drinking. His body was found in the harbor. He was wearing only his underwear.

▶ James Foley, a railroad employe, fell into the hold of a steamboat docked at Marquette, Michigan, on or about May 10. Witnesses said Foley fell twenty-five feet and landed on his head. After that, he walked to a doctor's office, got treatment, and then walked home. After reaching home he could not talk. He died a few hours later.

▶ Henry McGuinn, a deck hand on the propeller *St. Lawrence*, fell overboard and drowned off Kingston, Ontario, in the St. Lawrence River, on May 13.

▶ William Barry, a sailor on the schooner *M. Slavson*, fell overboard and drowned on July 9, five miles east of Big Summer Island. Barry was aloft furling the main topsail.

◗ John Leitch, lookout on the propeller *William Cowie*, drowned Saturday, July 13, while swimming in the St. Clair River while his ship was loading at St. Clair, Michigan.

◗ John Doyle, sailor aboard the schooner *Rising Star*, was killed when he fell from a small boat at Chicago about July 25.

◗ Thomas Jennings drowned when he fell from the barge *L. B. Crocker* at Port Colborne on Sunday, July 27. He was attempting to jump from the *Crocker* to another anchored vessel.

◗ John Herre, a passenger on the steamer *Marine City*, drowned in Lake Huron when he fell overboard on July 28.

◗ John Childs died when he fell from the deck of the brig *Harvest* at Cleveland, Ohio, on Monday, July 29.

◗ John Bassett drowned when he fell in Georgian Bay from the deck of the steamer *Chicora* late in July.

◗ Layman Bowers got caught in a wooden chute while iron ore was being dumped into the hold of the schooner *David Steward* at Escanaba on about August 1. The falling ore carried Bowers into the hold where he was partly buried. He was seriously hurt but lived.

◗ Tom Morgan, sailor on the steamer *Tioga*, died when a fender rope parted while he was hanging over the side of the ship off Long Point on Lake Erie on or about August 2. Morgan was attempting to enter the amidships gangway from outside the hull.

◗ Charles Smith, a crew member on the schooner *Willard*, drowned when he fell overboard near Chicago on Thursday, August 8.

◗ Capt. Elijah Blanchard, master of the schooner *Active*, drowned when he fell overboard while the ship was docked at Oswego, New York, on Saturday, August 10.

◗ Charles Hill of Racine, Wisconsin, was fatally injured when he fell into the hold of the schooner *Midnight* on Friday, August 16. The location of the accident was not recorded.

◗ Captain Waggoner, master of the barge *Severn*, fell from the deck to the dock, then fell into the water and drowned August 17 at Cleveland.

◗ Philip Nolan, first mate on the barge *Susan Ward*, drowned in Lake Erie when he fell overboard near Buffalo on Saturday, August 18. The barge was in a string of vessels in tow behind the steamer *Janness*, bound from Cleveland, Ohio.

❱ Michael Nenpert, fireman on the tug *H. A. Ballentine*, drowned at Bay City on Friday, August 22.

❱ Capt. Orrin Myrick was killed when he fell into the hold of the propeller *Neptune* at Cleveland on Monday, September 2.

❱ Sailors John Warwick and Malcolm McKay were killed when they both fell from the jib boom of the schooner *Tecumech*, near Spanish River, on Saturday, September 7.

❱ David Curran, mate of the schooner *Pearl*, fell from the deck and drowned in Lake Ontario on or about September 15.

❱ Deck hand Thomas Kelley was swept overboard from the tug *Crawford* near Chicago during a gale on or about September 18.

❱ Capt. R. P. Webster of Kingsville, Ohio, master of the propeller *Potomac*, drowned when he lost his footing and fell into the Detroit River on Sunday, September 22. Webster was helping attach a new fender to the side of the ship. When he tumbled, the fender went over with him and fell on top of him. He shouted from the water: "Stop her and back her," then "My back is broken."

❱ A second fatal accident occurred on the propeller *Tioga*. Sailor William Cherry fell overboard and drowned in Lake Erie on September 25. Cherry lost his balance while throwing a bucket of ashes over the rail. Tom Morgan fell overboard about August 1, also on Lake Erie.

❱ Captain Roache, master of the schooner *Harvest Home*, was killed on Sunday, October 6, when he fell forty feet from the ore dock at Marquette, Michigan, to the deck of his ship.

❱ A sailor named Murray fell from the jib boom of the schooner *Burnside* at Sarnia, Ontario, and drowned in the St. Clair River on October 11.

❱ Henry Ryder, a sailor on the schooner *Mollison*, was washed overboard on Lake Erie, near Port Colborne, on October 20.

❱ J. W. Harris fell from the deck of the steamer *Arizona* and drowned at Buffalo on or about October 26.

❱ Thomas Christopher, mate on the tug *Edsall*, sleep walked and fell overboard to drown in Kingston harbor on or about October 28.

▶ Sailors William Haven and Charles Albright were killed when they fell to the deck from aloft on the schooner *Elizabeth A. Nicholson* during a northwest gale. Haven and Albright were reefing the topsail when one of the men lost his hold and started to fall. In his panic he grabbed the other man and both tumbled to their death. The accident happened on November 25.

▶ J. Schefiner, first engineer, and an unnamed fireman on the propeller *Pittsburg* were drowned at Bay City, Michigan, on Friday, November 29.

*****

Capt. Paul Pelkey, master of the iron steamer *Ivanhoe*, responded to an announcement of his death in the *Chicago Times*: "The item in the *Times* announcing my death must be a mistake," he said.

The Final Counting

Shipping was a dangerous business in 1872. In addition to the lives lost, accidents, storms, fires and other disasters wrecked eight hundred sixty-three boats.

Of these wrecks, seventy-three ships were written off as total losses. They included the steamers *Kingston, Lac La Belle, China, Galena, Detroit, Dalhousie, John Stewart, Mary R. Robinson* and *Mary Ward*. Also lost were forty-five schooners, ten barges, eight scows and one brig. The total loss for the year added up to about twenty-two thousand tons.

In spite of the losses, the number of boats on the lakes increased. Shipbuilders were busy in 1872, replenishing the vessels that disappeared. Twenty-seven new steamships slid down the ways, as well as forty-four new sailing ships and five barges boasting a total shipping capacity of thirty-six thousand tons.

The largest of these new vessels included the sister ships *Cuba, Russia* and *Java*, all boasting thirteen hundred tons, each, and the *Montana*, with one thousand tons.

Bibliography:

Alpena Argus, 1872 editions, Michigan State Library microfilm file, Lansing, Mich.

Bay City Daily Journal, 1872 editions, Michigan State Library microfilm file, Lansing, Mich.

Beers, J. H. and Co., *History of the Great Lakes with Illustrations*, Volumes 1 and 2, Chicago, 1899.

Buffalo Courier, 1872 editions microfilm file, Buffalo Public Library, Buffalo, N.Y.

Buffalo Morning Express, 1872 editions, Buffalo Public Library microfilm file, Buffalo, N.Y.

Chicago Inter Ocean, 1872 editions, Central Library microfilm file, Chicago, Ill.

Chicago Inter Ocean, news clippings from 1876, 1877 and 1878, Institute for Great Lakes Research, Perrysburg, O.

Chicago Record-Herald, Bundy obituary, September 17, 1906, courtesy the Chicago Historical Society, Chicago, Ill.

Cleveland Plain Dealer, 1872 editions, Cleveland Public Library microfilm file, Cleveland, Ohio.

Commonwealth, The, Duluth, July 30, 1894 clipping, Institute for Great Lakes Research, Perrysburg, O.

Daily Dispatch, Erie, Pa., November 28, 1872 clipping, Institute for Great Lakes Research, Perrysburg, O.

Detroit Advertiser and Tribune, 1872 editions, Michigan State Library microfilm file, Lansing, Mich.

Detroit Daily Post, 1872 editions, Michigan State Library microfilm file, Lansing, Mich.

Detroit Free Press, 1872 editions, Detroit Public Library microfilm file, Detroit, Mich.

Detroit Free Press, news clips from 1894, Institute for Great Lakes Research, Perrysburg, O.

Duluth Daily News, June 10, 1890 clipping, Institute for Great Lakes Research, Perrysburg, O.

Duluth Evening Herald, 1872 editions, from news clip files, Institute for Great Lakes Research, Perrysburg, O.

Duluth News Tribune, 1894 news clippings, Institute for Great Lakes Research, Perrysburg, O.

Erie Gazette, 1872 editions, from microfilm files, Erie Public Library, Erie, Pa.

Escanaba Tribune, 1872 editions, Michigan State Library microfilm file, Lansing, Mich.

Grand Traverse Herald, 1872 editions, Michigan State Library microfilm file, Lansing, Mich.

History of Steam on the Erie Canal, Appeal for the Extension of the Act of April, 1871 "to Foster and Develop the Inland Commere of the Lake," Henry Boynton, January 1873, Evening Post Steam Presses, New York, furnished by New York Historical Society, New York, N.Y.

Huron County News, 1872 editions, Bad Axe Public Library, Bad Axe, Mich.

Holzman, Robert S., *The Romance of Firefighting,* "Boston's Fire of 1872," p 110, Bazona Books, N.Y., 1956.

Marquette Mining Journal, 1872 editions, Michigan State Library microfilm file, Lansing, Mich.

Milwaukee Sentinel, 1872 editions, Milwaukee Public Library, Milwaukee, Wis.

Milwaukee Weekly Chronicle, 1872 editions, Milwaukee Public Library, Milwaukee, Wis.

Muskegon Enterprise, 1872 editions, Michigan State Library microfilm file, Lansing, Mich.

Muskegon Weekly Chronicle, 1872 editions, Michigan State Library microfilm file, Lansing, Mich.

Northwestern Republican, May 23, 1872 clipping, Institute for Great Lakes Research, Perrysburg, O.

Port Huron Daily Times, 1872 editions, Michigan State Library microfilm file, Lansing, Mich.

Port Huron Weekly Times, 1872 editions, Michigan State library microfilm file, Lansing, Mich.

South Haven Sentinel, 1872 editions, Michigan State Library microfilm file, Lansing, Mich.

Telescope, September-October 1973, *The Lakes Unique Gospel Ship* by Charles H. Truscott, from Milwaukee Public Library, Milwaukee, Wis.

Toledo Blade, clippings found at the Institute for Great Lakes Research, Perrysburg, Ohio.

Toronto Daily Globe, 1872 editions, Sarnia Public Library microfilm file, Sarnia, Ontario.

Weekly Chronicle, Muskegon, Mich., 1872 editions, Michigan State Library microfilm file, Lansing, Mich.

STEAMBOATS IN ICE

Index of Vessels

Active, sch., captain drowned at Oswego, Aug. 10, p 174
Ada, scow, blown aground L Ontario, Sept. 29, p 126
Adriatic, bge, sunk L Erie gale, eight dead, Sept. 29, p 117
Agnes, scow, ashore L Erie, September 28, p 124
Ajax, barge, adrift in gale L Erie, Sept. 29, p 117
Ajax, str., burned Saginaw River, Aug. 7, p 74
Alaska, prop., operating L Michigan, May 6, p 50; aground Detroit River, Oct. 17, p 133
Algerian, ref. burned in 1905, p 54
Alice, tug, tows *Hawkins* to Grand Haven, Sept., p 97
Alleghaney, str., aground St. Clair Flats, May 6, p 50
Alpha, sch., aground L Ontario, Sept. 29, p 126
American Champion, sch., waterlogged L Erie, p 115
American Giant, bark, waterlogged L Erie, Jun. 4, p 45
Amoskeag, sch., operating L Erie, Oct. 28, p 135
Anderson, tug, operating at Buffalo, May, p 29
Anderson, Bob, tug, operating Duluth, Nov. 13, p 145
Antelope, sch., in ice at Oswego, N. Y., Apr. 13, p 10
Antelope, str., towed 8 barges St. Clair River, Jun., p 69
Arctic, str., frozen Portage Lake, Dec. 1, p 161
Argyle, prop., lost tow barges L Ontario, Sept. 29, p 123
Arizona, str., crew member drowned Buffalo, Oct., p 175; stranded in ice Sault Ste. Marie, Dec. 1, p 161
Atlantic, str., damaged in storm L Erie, Sept. 28, p 123; nearly lost in gale L Superior, Nov. 13, p 146; stranded in ice on Mud Lake, Dec. 1, p 161

Baker, A., scow, aground Cedar Pt., L Erie, Sept. 18, p 99
Baker, Timothy, sch., damaged by waterspout L Huron, Jun. 20, p 59
Balize, tug, towing lumber barges L Erie, Jun. 8, p 47; towed schooner *Joy* from L Erie gale, Nov. 29, p 157
Ballentine, H. A., tug, crew member drowned Bay City, Aug. 22, p 175
Baltic, barge, foundered L Erie gale, 7 dead, Sept. 29, p 117
Banner, barge, aground Toledo, Apr. 27, p 50
Barter, barge, adrift L Erie, Sept. 18, p 99
Bartlett, F. A., tug, involved in salvage work on Detroit River, p 42
Bavarian, burned L. Ontario, p 54
Bay City, barge, waterlogged L Erie, Sept. 18, p 97

179

STEAMBOATS IN ICE

Baxter, Wm, experimental steam barge Erie Canal, p 62
Bemis, Philo S., tug, burned Alpena, Sept. 15, p 96
Benton, prop., aground Tawas Bay, Sept. 29, p 122; picked up stranded sailors L Huron, Dec. 7, p 162; assisted stranded str. *Wenona*, Dec. 7, p 164
Bertschy, J., str., burned De Pere, Wis., Aug. 25, p 79; aground Escanaba, Mich., Nov. 27, p 160
Bissell, Harvey, bge, collision Saginaw River, May 27, p 36
Black Duck, sloop, sunk L Ontario, Jul. 26, p 72
Board of Trade, bark, aground L Erie, Nov. 28, p 159
Booth, Mary, bark, aground Green Bay, Sept. 28, p 125
Braley, barge, adrift L Erie, Sept. 18, p 99
Breden, John, bark, capt. drowned Buffalo, May 9, p 173
Brockway, tug, working at Port Huron, Jun. 15, p 57
Brooklyn, str., caught in ice L Ontario, Apr. 22, p 16
Brown, Hattie T., ferry, sunk in collision Saginaw River, Oct. 10, p 127
Brown, Tom, tug, operating L Mich., Sept. 28, p 108
Brown, William O., sch., rescued crew of capsized *Meeker*, Aug. 28, p 81; sunk with all hands L Superior, Nov. 27, p 160
Bruce, Kate L., aground L Erie, Nov. 28, p 159
Butcher Boy, bark, sunk L Erie, Sept. 28, p 123
Burlington, steam barge, lost barges L Erie storm, Nov. 7, p 141; sunk by ice Point au Pelee, L Erie, Nov. 29, p 155
Burnside, sch., crew member killed Sarnia, Ont., Oct. 11, p 175
Butts, C. C., sch., waterlogged L Michigan, Sept. 28, p 125

Cambridge, bark, stranded in ice Sault Ste. Marie, Dec. 1, p 161
Camden, sch., launched Cleveland, April 20, p 30
Campbell, Colin, str., lost barges L Huron, Sept. 28, p 116
Canisteo, str., chief engineer killed in fight, Jul., p 67; in ice at Cleveland, Dec. 1, p 165
Cascade, sch., aground L Superior, Jun. 9, p 52
Case, Lydia, bark, ashore L Michigan, Sept. 28, p 125
Cecilia, bark, aground S. Manitou Island, Sept. 28, p 124
Centurion, sch., rescued crew L Ontario, Nov. 12, p 144
Challenge, sch., stranded L Michigan, Oct. 12, p 171
Chambers, Annie Belle, sch., capsized Toronto, Sept. 29, p 126
Champion, tug, towed eight barges on St. Clair River, Jul. 3, p 69; burned Detroit, Jul. 18, p 71
Champlain, prop., breaks through ice Straits of Mackinac, Apr. 28, p 21; last try to break ice L St. Clair, Dec. 9, p 168

STEAMBOATS IN ICE

Cherubusco, scow, aground Death's Door, L Michigan, Sept. 28, p 125; wrecked L Michigan, Nov. 16, p 172

Chicago, prop., sunk in ice Buffalo, May 13, p 27; rescued crew of *Mitchell*, L Michigan, Nov. 25, p 148

Chicora, str., crew member drowned G. Bay, July, p 174

China, str. [American] operating L Superior, Nov. 28, p 153

China, str., [Canadian] launched Kingston, Ont., Apr. 27, p 31; burned L Ontario, Oct. 14, p 128

Citizen, sch., picked up crew of *D. L. Couch* L Erie, July 19, p 72; on L Superior in Nov. gale, p 153

City of Boston, str., in ice L Ontario, Apr. 22-28, p 17; rescued *Corsair* crew, L Huron, Sept. gale, p 109; last try to get through ice L St. Clair, Dec. 9, p 168

City of Buffalo, bark, aground St. Clair River, Aug. 29, p 83

City of Concord, prop., rescued crew of *Dalhousie* L Ontario, Sept. 26, p 101

City of Erie, bge, adrift in storm L Michigan, Sept. 28, p 107

City of Fremont, prop., operating northern L Michigan, July 29, 73; pulled *Equinox* off S. Manitou Is., Sept. gale, p 124; in collision with sch. *Lummis*, Oct. 5, p 126

City of London, str., in storm L Ontario, Aug. 29, p 83

City of Madison, prop., in storm L Superior, Aug. 29, p 83

Clayton, canal boat operating at Cleveland, July 17, p 68

Cleveland, H. G., sch., capsized L Huron, Nov. 6, p 140

Cobb, Ahira, sch., launched at Cleveland, May 13, p 30

Cochrane, Neil, scow, aground L Michigan, Sept. 28, p 126

Coe, S. S., tug, involved in Lake Erie salvage, p 40

Colonel Ellsworth, bark, ashore L Erie, Jun., p 46

Colorado, barge, adrift in gale L Huron, Sep. 28, p 116

Commerce, brig, rescued survivors of *Fearless* L Michigan, Aug. 8, p 74

Compound, tug, exploded Buffalo, one killed, May 10, p 24

Cone, Eva M., sch., capsized and beached, Port Washington, Wis., Apr. 22, p 15

Cooke, Jay, str., caught in floating lumber Detroit River, Sept. 28, p 114

Corlet, Minnie, scow, ashore Pentwater, Mich., one dead, Nov. 27, p 160

Corning, Erastus, bark, dragging bottom at Chicago, Apr. 27, p 49; attempted rescue L Huron, Sept. gale, p 104

Corsair, sch., sunk L Huron, six dead, Sept. 28, p 109

Couch, D. L., sch., sunk L Erie, July 22, p 72

Couch, James, barge, grounded St. Clair Flats, struck by another vessel, Oct. 14, p 52

Cowie, William, prop, crew member killed on St. Clair River,

181

July 13, p 174
> *Craig, Alice,* sch., aground Duluth, Nov. 13, p 145
> *Craig, Annie L.,* prop., lost barges L Erie, Sept. 18, p 99
> *Crawford,* tug, deck hand drowned Chicago, Sept. 18, p 175
> *Crawford, R. C.,* sch., hit by lightning L Erie, Sept. 5, p 91
> *Crocker, L. B.,* barge, crew member killed, Jul. 27, p 174
> *Crusader,* tug, salvage St. Lawrence River, June, p 48
> *Cuba,* prop., new iron carrier launched, p 30; dragged bottom at St. Clair Flats on first trip, Jun. 12, p 51
> *Cumberland,* str., took passengers from *Manitoba,* L Superior, Jul., p 66
> *Cushing, W. D.,* tug, rescued *Middlesex* crew, Nov. 27, p 154
> *Cuyahoga,* str., in ice at Sault Ste. Marie, Dec. 1, p 161
> *Czar,* sch., collision on St. Clair River, May 6, p 50
>
> *Dalhousie,* prop., burned L Ontario, Sept. 26, p 101
> *Danforth, F. L.,* tug, burned Duluth, Aug. 9, p 75
> *Dart, Russell,* sch., sunk in ice at Port Colborne, Ont., p 29
> *Day Spring,* sch., hit by lightning, one dead, Aug. 14, p 77
> *Delaware,* sch., stranded on L Michigan, Nov. 27
> *Detroit,* barge, collision on Saginaw River, May 27, p 36
> *Detroit,* prop., wrecked Saginaw Bay, Sept. 29, p 119
> *Dix, John A.,* str., lost barges *Jupiter* and *Saturn* L Superior, Nov. 27, p 152; in ice at Sault Ste. Marie, Dec. 1, p 161
> *Dobbins, D. P.,* sch., collision at St. Clair Flats, Oct. 14, p 52; struck by crew at Buffalo, Sept., p 94
> *Dolphin,* sch., salvaged by Capt. Danger, p 38
> *Dominion,* prop., rescued survivors of *Kingston* fire, St. Lawrence River, June 11, p 54
> *Donnelly, John,* tug, p 54
> *Dormer, Grace,* burned Beaver Island, L Michigan, one dead, Jul. 2, p 63
> *Dove,* str., burned at Amherstburg, Ont., June 4, p 45
> *Dragon,* tug, rescue at Erie, Nov. 27, p 155
> *Drake, Ben,* tug, operating at Chicago, April 15, p 13; rescued crew of *Cherubusco,* Nov., p 172
> *Drake, John H.,* sch., wrecked L Michigan, Sept. 28, p 107
> *Dunkirk,* str., in storm L Erie, Sept. 18, p 97
>
> *Eagle Wing,* sch., nearly capsized, Sept. 28, p 123
> *East Saginaw,* str., p 37.
> *Edsall,* tug, mate drowned at Kingston, Oct. 28, p 175
> *Eldorado,* barge, grounded L Mich., April 14, p 49
> *Elgin, William,* sch., aground L Ontario, Nov. 28, p 161
> *Elliott, R. R.,* barge, wrecked L Erie, Sept. 18, p 97

STEAMBOATS IN ICE

Elva, str., formerly the *Glad Tidings*, p. 87
Ely, George H., barge, grounded St. Clair Flats, May 6, p 50
Emerald, barge, adrift in gale L Huron, Sept. 28, p 116
Empire, str., in ice L Ontario, April 22-28, p 16
Ensign, canal boat at Cleveland, captain murdered, July 17, p 68
Equinox, str., aground S. Manitou Is., Sept. 28, p 124
Erie, sch., sunk L Erie, August 29, p 82
Escanaba, sch., in L Superior ice, Dec. 1, p 163
Evaline, sch., collision on St. Clair River, May 6, p 50
Evergreen City, prop., salvaged L Erie, July, p 41
Exile, sch., ashore L Superior, Nov. 13, p 146

Farwell, sch., in ice on Mud Lake, Dec. 1, p 161
Favorite, tug, salvage work on Detroit River, p 42; collision on L Michigan, Aug. 16, p 77
Fay, Joseph S., str., frozen in Lake Superior, Dec. 1, p 163
Fayette, str., salvaged, p 37
Fearless, sch., capsized L Michigan, Aug. 8, p 74
Ferry, Thomas W., sch., launched April 16, Detroit, p 30
Fisk, James Jr., str., in ice at Cleveland, Dec. 1, p 165
Floretta, sch., picked up *Lac La Belle* survivors, L Michigan, Sept. 15, p 132
Flying Mist, bark, docked at Chicago, April 15, p 13
Forest City, prop., operating on St. Clair River, Oct. 14, p 51
Forester, barge, wrecked L Erie, Sept. 18, p 97
Forest Maid, scow, collision on L Erie, May 8, p 23
Forest Queen, barge, sunk L Erie, five dead, Nov. 7, p 141
Fountain City, experimental steam barge Erie Canal, p 62
Fountain City, prop., in storm L Michigan, Sept. 28, p 124
Fulton, sch., sunk Saginaw River, May 19, p 34

Galena, prop., wrecked Thunder Bay, Sept. 24, p 102
Gardner, tug, located lost barges L Erie, Nov. 8, p 142
General Burnside, tug, at Port Huron, June 15, p 57
Gibbs, R. J., ashore L Erie, Sept. 28, p 124
Gladiator, tug, pulled record eleven barges , June, p 69
Glad Tidings, sch., Great Lakes Gospel Ship, p 84; rescues crew of *Hawkins*, Sept. 17, p 97
Globe, barge, aground at Tawas Point, Sept. 28, p 123
Goble, George, sch., released from ice L Huron, Apr. 12, p 9
Golden Rule, sch., wrecked L Superior, Nov. 27, p 160
Gould, John, str., grounded St. Clair Flats, Nov., p 52
Graham, Jennie, sch., capsized L Huron, April 24, p 18
Grandy, H., sch., crew member hurt, April 12, p 173

STEAMBOATS IN ICE

Granite State, prop., collision L Erie, May 8, p 23
Grant, W. M., sch., ashore L Erie, Nov. 27, p 159
Graves, W. T., str., grounded St. Clair Flats, May, p 50
Griswold, C. C., sch., sunk L Superior, eight dead, Nov. 26, p 172

Hamilton, sch., capsized L Michigan, Nov. 6, p 140
Hanson, scow, collision at Port Huron, Mich., July 5, p 64
Harvest, brig, crew member killed Cleveland, July 29, p 174
Harvest Home, sch., captain killed in fall Oct. 6, p 175
Hathaway, Col., sch., in storm L Erie, Sept. 28, p 124
Hawkins, W. H., sch., trouble L Michigan, Sept. 17, p 97
Hector, tug, operating L Erie, p 124
Heg, Colonel, sch., ashore L Michigan, Sept. 28, p 126
Hemje, C., experimental steam barge on Erie Canal, p 62
Hercules, tug, involved in salvage work, p 38
Higby, Len, sch., aground L Michigan, Mar., p 171
Hippogriffe, sch., carrying gunpowder in thunderstorm, L Erie, Sept. 5, p 92
Home, sch., in gale L Michigan, Dec. 4, p 166
Hornet, sch., in rescue, L. Superior, Sept., p 126
Howe, William, bark, aground L Ontario, Sept. 29, p 123
Hoyt, Jesse, bark, storm L Huron, Sept. 28, p 123
Hunter, barge, aground on Saginaw Bay, one dead, Sept. 29, p 119
Hurd, J. L., prop., aground L St. Clair, June 22, p 51
Huron City, prop., rescued *Erie* crew L Erie, Aug. 29, p 82

International, railroad ferry, launched July 17, p 30
Iron City, barge, sunk L Erie, Sept. 25, p 105
Isabel, barge, in storm L Huron, Sept. 28, p 116
Isabella, tug, burned Toronto Sept. 3, p 171
Ivanhoe, str., operating at Chicago, p 176

Jackson, Andrew, U.S. Revenue Cutter, saved crew of *York State*, Milwaukee, Sept. 29, p 113
Jamaica, sch., capsized L Huron, one dead, June 20, p 58
Japan, str., in ice at Sault Ste. Marie, December 1, p 161
Jarecki, Mary, str., grounded on Summer Is., Green Bay, Oct. 24, p 172
Java, new iron freighter launched, p 30; record load of grain carried, June, p 69; docked at Cleveland for winter, Dec. 1, p 166
Jeffery, Celia, sch., storm L Erie, Nov. 30, p 158; moored at Cleveland, Dec. 1, p 165
Jenness, prop., towed *Sweepstakes* to Port Huron, Mich.,

STEAMBOATS IN ICE

14, p 56; operating on L Erie, Aug. 18, p 175; towed *Sweepstakes* through severe gale, Sept. 28, p 123

Jennie and Annie, sch., crew member killed L Erie, May 6, p 173; wrecked L Michigan, three or more drowned, Nov. 6, p 139

John, William, sch., sunk L Ontario, Nov. 12, p 144

Johnston, Hattie, sch., ashore Straits, Sept. 28, p 125

Jones, C. W., tug, cut by ice L Erie, May 11, p 29

Jones, Elizabeth, sch., collision L Erie, Nov. 11, p 144

Jones, Mary E., sch., struck by crew at Buffalo, p 94

Jones, William, sch., rescue of stranded sailors, Manistee, Mich., April 14, p 12; waterlogged L Michigan, Apr. 15, p 13

Joseph, barge, adrift in gale L Erie, Sept. 29, p 117

Josephine, sch., collisions Saginaw River, May 27, p 36

Joy, James F., sch., storm L Erie, Nov. 29, p 156

Jupiter, barge, sunk L Superior, crew killed, Nov. 27, p 151

Kanter, Edward, sch., wrecked L Michigan, Nov. 27, p 160

Kelley, Fred, barge, operating on Green Bay, Oct. 24, p 172

Kentucky, barge, storm L Erie, Nov. 7, p 141

Kimball, sch., in ice on Mud Lake, December 1, p 161

King, James C., bark, operating at Chicago, Apr. 15, p 13; ashore in Green Bay, Sept. 28, p 125

Kingston, str., burns St. Lawrence River, one dead, Jun. 11, p 53

Lac La Belle, prop., attempted to save drifting *Lake Michigan*, L Michigan, Sept. 28, p 121; sunk L Michigan, eight dead, Oct. 14, p 128

Lake Breeze, prop., operating L Huron, Apr. 17, p 49; burns L Huron, Aug. 26, p 78

Lake Michigan, str., storm L Michigan, Sept. 28, p 121

Lawrence, prop., in ice L Ontario, Apr. 22-28, p 16; last try in ice on Lake St. Clair, Dec. 9, p 168

Lawrence, Josephine, collision L Michigan, Aug. 16, p 76

Lewis, Daniel, str., in ice Sault Ste. Marie, Dec. 1, p 161

Leviathan, tug, salvage work, p 38; salvaged *Mary Robinson* hull, July, p 73; working to save *York State* L Michigan, Sept. 28, p 113; pulled *Richmond* off rocks Cross Village, p 124; pulled *Jarecki* off Summer Island, Oct., p 172

Liberty, sch., wrecked at Milwaukee pier, Apr. 14, p 11

Lincoln, A., barge, ashore L Huron, Sept. 28, p 123

Lind, Jenny, sch., waterlogged L Michigan, Sept. 28, p 125

Little May, barge, adrift L Erie, Sept. 18, p 99

Louisa, scow, capsized L Huron, Sept. 18, p 99

Lummis, B. R., sch., collision L Michigan, Oct. 5, p 126

185

Mackinaw, str., involved in salvage of *Merchant*, May, p 41
Magnet, tug, salvage work, p 38; attempted to salvage barges caught in ice, L Erie, Nov., p 158
Mail, sch., ashore L Ontario, Apr. 27, p 171
Maine, prop., sunk on St. Lawrence River, June 9, p 48
Major Dana, tug, operating on L Erie, p 10
Manistee, prop., in ice at Grand Haven, Mich., p 8; collision L Michigan, May 24, p 35
Manitoba, str., aground L Superior, July 11, p 65
Maplebranch, Canadian vessel, p. 30
Maple Leaf, sch., aground L Superior, Sept. 28, p 126
Marine City, str., passenger lost L Huron, July 28, p 174
Mariner, barge, adrift L Erie, Sept. 18, p 99
Mariner, str., operating on St. Clair River, Nov., p 52
Marquette, sch., saved from sinking by a fish, May 18, p 32; ashore L Superior, Nov. 27, p 160
Martin, D. R., sch., waterlogged L Michigan, Sept. 28, p 125
Martin, S. H., tug, working at Port Huron, Mich., p 9
Maxwell, sch., aground in St. Clair Flats, Aug. 29, p 83
May, Lillie, barge, adrift L. Erie, p 99
McGlivra, Nellie, barge, waterlogged L Erie, Sept. 18, p 99
McGregor, Wm., bge, grounded St. Clair Flats, Oct. 14, p 51
McLane, tug, working at Chicago, April 15, p 13
Meeker, Louis, sch., capsized L Michigan, Aug. 28, p 79
Mendota, str., operating on L Erie, June 4, p 46; caught in Sept. gale, p 99
Menomonee, prop., launched at Menomonee, Mich., Sept. 7, p 31; in ice L Superior, Dec. 1, p 161
Merchant, prop., aground on Detroit River, May 20, p 40
Messenger, prop., in ice L Michigan, April 14, p 12
Metropolis, sch., frozen in Mud Lake, December 1, p 161
Michigan, US gunboat, operating on L Erie, Nov. 27, p 155
Middlesex, sch., grounded L Superior, Nov. 27, p 154
Midnight, sch., crew member killed, Aug. 10, p 174; aground in Straits, Sept. 18, p 99
Mills, M. I., tug, burned at Amherstburg, Ont., Mar. 1, p 8; lost barge *Iron City* L Erie, Sept. 25, p 105
Milwaukee, str., in ice L Ontario, April 22-28, p 16
Mineral Rock, str., in gale L. Superior, Nov. 13, p 146
Minor, John, sch., struck by crew at Buffalo, p 94
Mitchell, Minot, sch., sunk L Michigan, Nov. 25, p 148
Moffatt, Kate, tug, salvage Saginaw Bay, Sept., p 120
Mollison, sch., crew member drowned L Erie, Oct. 20, p 175
Monitor, tug, stuck in mud Muskegon, Aug. 29, p 81
Montana, prop., bad launch at Port Huron, June 15, p 56

Montank, sch., aground L Huron, Aug. 29, p 83
Montezuma, brig, sank all hands L Erie, Sept. 29, p 120
Moore, William A., tug, rescue L Erie, May 13, p 28; in gale L Erie, lost barge tow, Sept. 29, p 117
Morning Star, barge, in ice Lake Erie, Nov. 30, p 158
Morning Star, sch., capsized L Michigan, Nov 27, p 160
Morning Star, str., operating Saginaw River, Oct. 10, p 127
Morse, Fred A., sch., grounded St. Clair Flats, Nov. 21, p 52
Moss, A. H., sch., storm at Marquette, Sept. 28, p 126
Mountaineer, sch., wrecked L. Huron, Oct. 15, p 171
Mueller, Minnie, sch., lost with all hands, probably in Lake Huron, September gale, p 122
Mystic, tug, operating Sandusky, Ohio, May 8, p 24

Narragausett, sch., ashore Straits, Sept. 28, p 123
Nashua, prop., salvage at Straits, Sept., p 125
Nau, Libbie, barge, collision L Huron, Sept. 28, p 112
Nau, Mary, sch., sank L Michigan, Sept. 28, p 124
Neptune, prop., captain killed at Cleveland, Sept. 22, p 175
Neshoto, sch., sunk L Huron, two survivors, Sept. 29, p 122
New Dominion, sch., rescued crew, July 29, p 73
New Era, prop., lost barges L Michigan, Sept.28, p 107
New Hampshire, sch., collision L Michigan, Nov. 18, p 148
Newman, William, experimental str. Erie Canal, p 62
Nicholson, Elizabeth A., sch., sailors killed, Nov. 25, p 176
North Star, sch., ashore Pentwater, Mich., Nov. 27, p 160
Northwest, bark, ashore L Huron, Nov. 27, p 161
Norman, str., in ice L Superior, Dec. 1, p 161

Oak Leaf, sch., frozen L Superior, Dec. 1, p 163
Ocean, barge, sunk in ice L Erie, May, p 29; sunk in L Erie storm, Aug. 29, p 82
Ocean, prop., operating on L Erie, May 13, p 28
Ogden, W. B., sch., frozen L Superior, Dec. 1, p 163
Ontario, barge, adrift L Erie, Sept. 18, p 99; waterlogged L Huron, Sept. 29, p 118; sunk, crew killed, L Erie gale, Nov 30, p 158
Orion, sch., sunk L Erie, Aug. 29, p 82
Oswegatchie, str., in ice L Ontario, April 22-28, p 16
Ottawa, sch., at Erie, Pa., Nov. 27, p 155; sunk with all hands L Erie, Nov. 30, p 158

Palms, Francis, sch., aground Duluth, Nov. 13, p 145
Paragon, sch., finds wreck of *Rapid* L Erie, Sept., p 94
Pathfinder, sch., aground L Huron, Aug. 29, p 83
Pearl, sch., first mate killed L Ontario, Sept. 15, p 175

Peck, E. M., tug, salvage of *Manitoba* L Superior, July, p 66
Peerless, prop., launched at Cleveland, June 8, p 30; in ice Sault Ste. Marie, Dec. 1, p 161
Perew, Frank, tug, recovered barge L Erie, Sept., p 99
Pittsburg, prop., sailors drowned Bay City, Nov. 29, p 176
Planet, barge, wrecked L Michigan, Nov. 7, p 172
Plymouth, barge, in storm L Huron, Sept. 28, p 116
Potomac, sch., Capt. Bundy's early command, p 84
Potomac, prop., captain drowned Detroit, Sept. 22, p 175
Powhattan, brig, collision on St. Clair River, May 6, p 50
Pratt, P. P., tug, boiler explosion L Ontario, Oct. 25, p 135
Prince of Wales, bark, ashore L Ontario, Sept. 29, p 123
Prindiville, John, tug, working in ice Straits of Mackinac, April 28, p 21; salvage at Port Huron, June, p 57; lost tow barges L Huron, Sept. 28, p 112; salvage of *Burlington*, Nov., p 156
Pringle, Wm. H., tug, on Saginaw River, May 27, p 36

Quayle, tug, salvage of *Manitoba* L Superior, July, p 66; salvaged bark *Northwest*, Nov., p 161

Ransom, James T., tug, collision Saginaw River, p. 36; capsized Niagara River, two killed, June 8, p 47; collision Saginaw River, Oct. 10, p 127
Rapid, sch., capsized L Erie, seven dead, Sept. 13, p 94
Rebecca, sch., ashore Tawas City, Sept. 28, p 123
Red, White and Blue, sch., rescued captain of *Iron City*, Sept. 25, p 106
Rescue, tug, salvage work, p 38; raised *Jamaica* L Huron, June, p 59; attempted salvage *Detroit* Saginaw Bay, Sept., p 120
Reynolds, George W., str., burned Bay City., Nov. 27, p 151
Rhodes, D. P., barge, grounded St. Clair Flats, May 6, p 50; record load of ore carried, Aug., p 70
Richardson, sch., aground Presque Isle, Aug. 29, p 83
Richmond, H. A., sch., stranded l. Mich., Sept. 28, p 124
Rio Grande, sch., aground Erie, Pa., Nov. 27, p 154
Rising Star, sch., sailor killed at Chicago, July 25, p 174
Ritchie, barge, storm L Huron, Sept. 28, p 116; in ice L Erie, Nov. 30, p 158
Roberts, E. C., sch., scuttled Marquette, Sept. 28, p 126
Robinson, Mary R., str., burned Straits,, July 29, p 73
Robinson, Sam, sch., collision, L Michigan, May 24, p 35
Rochester, str., passenger drowned L Ontario, May 8, p 173
Rooney, Henry, brig, salvaged L Erie, p 40
Ross, Harriet, sch., docked Chicago, April 15, p 13

STEAMBOATS IN ICE

Russell, George D., sch., operating L Erie, May, p 50
Russia, prop., new iron steamer launched, p 30

Saginaw, sch., docked at Duluth, Aug. 9, p. 75
St. Albans, str., battle ice L St. Clair, Dec. 9, p 168
St. Andrews, sch., collision L St. Clair, Sept. 26, p 171
St. Clair, barge, waterlogged Lake Huron, Aug. 29, p 83
St. Lawrence, prop., deck hand drowned, May 13, p 173
St. Lewis, str., in ice Sault Ste. Marie, Dec. 1, p 161
St. Paul, str., in storm Duluth, Nov. 13, p 145; in ice Mud Lake, Dec. 1, p 161
Samson, tug, involved in salvage work, p 38
Sandusky, prop., storm L. Huron, Sept. 29, p 118
Sargent, J. W., sch., late arrival Detroit, Sept. 6, p 92; caught in ice and sunk on Lake Erie, Nov. 30, p 158
Saturn, barge, lost with crew L Superior, Nov. 27, p 151
Schupe, William, sch., frozen L Superior, Dec. 1, p 163
Scotia, prop., new iron steamer launched, p 30
Scott, tug, operating at Cleveland, November, p 157
Scott, Thomas A., str., grounded St. Clair Flats, Nov., p 52
Severn, barge, captain killed Cleveland, Aug. 17, p 174
Sheldon, S. C., str., storm on L Erie, Nov. 29, p 156
Sheppard, L. B., sch., fire L Michigan, Sept., p 93
Sheridan, Phil., prop., crew member drowned Detroit, April 12, p 173; in gale on Saginaw Bay, Sept. 27, p 107
Sherwood, Annie, sch., operating on L Erie, May, p 50
Silver Spray, tug, salvage Isle Royal Sept. gale, p 126
Slavson, M., sch., crew member drowned, July 9, p 173
Smith, H. P., tug, burned Saginaw River, May 27, p 171
Somerset, barge, collision L Erie, May 11, p 24
Southwest, barge, aground L Huron, Sept. 28, p 112
Souvenir, sch., ashore L Michigan, crew lost, Nov. 27, p 160
Stanley, Joseph, canal boat at Cleveland, July 17, p 68
Starlight, sch., operating on L Huron, June 20, p 59
Star of the North, sch., capsized L Erie, May 11, p 171; cut adrift Lake Erie gale, Nov. 7, p 141
Steward, David, sch., crew member hurt, Aug. 1, p 174; collision St. Clair Flats, Aug. 29, p 83
Stewart, John, str., burned Saginaw Bay, Nov. 17, p 147
Stranger, tug, operating on St. Clair River, May, p 51
Sunrise, fishing tender, capsized Cleveland, Nov. 28, p 157
Sweepstakes, barge, damaged by September storm, page 123

Sweepstakes, sch., rescue L Michigan, April 24, p 19; waterlogged Saginaw Bay, June 14, p 56; in gale L Huron, Sept. 28, p 123
Sweepstakes, tug, salvage of *Merchant,* May, p 41; towed *Wenona* to Detroit, Dec. 7, p 164
Sweetheart, sch., ashore Duluth, Nov. 13, p 145
Sweet Home, sch., sunk St. Lawrence River, Sept. 18, p 99

Table Rock, barge, wrecked L. Huron, Sept. 29, p 118
Tarrant, Robert, tug, saved crew of *Wm. Jones* near Chicago, April 15, p 13
Taylor, Mary, sch., in ice L. Ontario, April 13, p 10
Tecumech, sch., two crew members killed, Sept. 7, p 175
Thompson, Maggie, sch., collision L Mich., Nov. 18, p 148
Tioga, str., crew member killed L Erie, Aug. 2, p 174; second fatal accident, Sept. 25, p 175
Toledo, str., collision at Port Huron, July 5, p 64
Torrent, tug, salvage work, p 38; lost string of barges L Erie, Nov. 30, p 158
Treat, William, barge, aground Bar Point, Sept. 28, p 124
Trusdell, str., in ice L Superior, Dec. 1, p 161

Union, prop., aground L Superior, June 9, p 52
Urania, tug, salvage work L St. Clair, June, p 51

Vanderbilt, str., grounded St. Clair Flats, Nov., p 52
Van Valkenburg, Lucinda, sch., waterspout L Huron, June 20, p 59
Vought, Annie, sch., collision L Erie, Sept. 28, p 123
Vulcan, tug, salvage work, p. 38; at Port Huron, June 15, p 57; lost lumber raft at Port Hope, Sept. 28, p 113

Wadsworth, tug, battling ice at Buffalo, May 10, p 25
Wanderer, sch., aground Detroit River, salvaged, p 41
Ward, Mary, operating L Ontario, Sept. 26, p 101; wrecked Georgian Bay, eight dead, Nov. 25, p 149
Ward, Susan, barge, mate drowned L Erie, Aug. 18, p 174
Warner, John F., barge, gale L Erie, Nov. 30, p 158
Waurecan, barge, adrift L Huron, Sept. 28, p 116
Wenona, prop., in ice at Alpena, April 22, p 14; operating on L Huron, p 103; broken rudder L Huron, Dec. 7, p 164
White Oak, sch., murder at Welland Canal, Oct. 14, p 133
White Squall, barge, collision L Huron, Sept. 28, p 112
Whitney, G. J., sch., aground Vermillion, O., Aug. 29, p 82; lost with all hands L Michigan, Sept. 28, p 108
Wilcox, tug, in salvage work L St. Clair, June, p 51

Wilcox, M. S., sch., collision L. St. Clair, Sept. 26, p 171
Willard, sch., crew member drowned Chicago, Aug. 8, p 174
Williams, Eliza, tug, engine trouble L Erie, Oct. 28, p 135
Willis, sch., collision L Erie, Nov. 11, p 144
Winslow, tug, salvaging on Great Lakes, p 37
Wolverine, barge, collision L Erie, May 11, p 24

Yankee Blade, sch., aground L Erie, Sept. 28, p 124
York State, sch., wrecked Milwaukee, Sept. 28, p 113
Young America, str., in ice L Superior, Apr., p 16
Young, Annie, prop., operating on L Huron, May 18, p 32
Young, William, sch., in ice L Erie, May, p 29

Zouave, tug, towing barges L Erie, May 11, p 24; loses barges L Huron, Sept. 29, p 118

Harbor scene showing grain elevators and steamer unloading grain at Buffalo. From Loudon G. Wilson Collection, Institute for Great Lakes Research

Glossary of Nautical Terms

Aft: The rear, or stern end of a ship.

Anchor: A heavy object attached to a ship by chain or cable, which, when thrown overboard, will hold the vessel in place.

Barge: A roomy, sometimes flat-bottomed vessel designed to carry bulk cargo. It can move under sail, be towed, or be powered by an engine. Schooners and other sailing ships were called barges when they were under tow.

Bark: A three-masted sailing ship with foremast and mainmast square rigged, and mizzenmast fore-and-aft rigged.

Barkentine: A three-masted sailing ship with foremast square rigged and the other two masts fore-and-aft rigged.

Boom: A long spar used to extend the bottom of a sail.

Bow: The front or forward part of a ship.

Bowsprit: A spar projecting forward from the stem of a ship.

Bridge: A platform erected above and across the deck of a ship from where the vessel is operated.

Bulkhead: Any partition separating compartments of a ship.

Bulwark: The side of a ship above the upper deck.

Buoy: A floating marker anchored in water to show locations of channels or sunken obstacles.

Fore-and-aft: In reference to sails of a ship, the canvas runs in the general line of the length of the vessel. Also located in, at or toward both the bow and stern of the ship.

Forecastle: The forward part of a ship where sailors live.

Foremast: The mast nearest to the bow of a vessel.

Foresail: The lowest sail on the foremast of a square-rigged ship; also the lower sail set on the foremast of a schooner.

Fore-topmast: A mast next above the foremast.

Founder: The sinking of a ship.

Galley: Kitchen of a ship.

Gangway: A door in the side or on a bulkhead of a ship.

Hatch: An opening on a ship's deck.

Hawser: A thick rope or cable used in pulling or anchoring or mooring a ship.

Hold: The interior of a ship below the lower deck where cargo is stowed.

Hook: Anchor.

Jib: A triangular sail extending from the head of the foremast to the bowsprit or jib boom.

Jib boom: A spar or boom used to extend the bowsprit on a sailing ship.

Life boat: A small boat on a ship used to escape in case of trouble.

Lighter: A large, flat-bottomed boat or scow used to carry cargo across shallow water to and from a ship.

Mainmast: The principal mast on a ship.

Mainsail: The principal sail on the mainmast.

Mainstay: The stay or supporting rope or wire connected from the maintop forward, usually to the foot of the foremast.

Mast: A long pole or spar rising from the keel of a ship to support sails, booms and rigging.

Mizzenmast: The aftermost mast in a two-masted or three-masted sailing vessel. When the vessel has four or more masts, it is the third mast from the bow.

Pilot: The person who steers a ship.

Pilothouse (or wheelhouse): The place on a ship where the pilot steers the vessel.

Propeller: A motorized vessel driven through the water by propellers.

Port: The left side of a ship to someone looking forward toward the bow.

Porthole: An opening or window in the side of a ship.

Reef: A chain of rocks or earth lying near the surface of the water. Also used as a verb which means reducing the amount of working canvass on a sailing ship.

Rigging: The ropes and pulleys that support and control a ship's sails, masts and spars. Also a word used to describe the design of a ship.

Schooner: A sailing ship with fore and aft rigging.

Scow: A large flat-bottomed boat with broad, square ends.

Side-wheeler (or side-wheel steamer): A steam powered vessel propelled through the water by large paddle wheels mounted on the sides.

Starboard: The right side of a ship to a person looking forward toward the bow.

Steamboat (or steamer, steamship): Any vessel powered by a steam engine. In old accounts, most commonly used for ships propelled by side-mounted paddle wheels.

Stern: The rear, or aft end of a ship.

Superstructure: The cabins, pilot house and other buildings erected above the main deck of a ship.

Tug (or tugboat): A ship with powerful engines designed for towing.

Waterlogged: The condition of a wooden ship in a sinking condition, but buoyed up by a cargo of material that is lighter than water.

James Donahue

About the Author:

James L. Donahue was born June 1, 1938 at Harbor Beach, Michigan. He discovered an interest in writing in high school and took a part-time job on the *Harbor Beach Times.* While in college, Donahue took a year off from his studies to work for the *Huron Daily Tribune,* Bad Axe, Michigan. Following graduation from Central Michigan University with majors in Journalism and English literature, Donahue went to work for the former *News-Palladium* in Benton Harbor, Michigan, worked two years at the *Kalamazoo Gazette,* Kalamazoo, Michigan, and finally became Sanilac County bureau chief for the *Times Herald,* Port Huron, Michigan, in 1971. He retired in 1993 to found Anchor Publications, a family-owned publishing business involved in literary and historical writing and research.

Donahue writes a syndicated weekly column for the *Times Herald,* the *Mining Journal,* Marquette, Mich., and the *Huron Daily Tribune,* Bad Axe, Mich., about shipwrecks and other historical events on the lakes. His stories also have appeared in the *Grand Rapids Press* and the *Traverse City Record Eagle.* In 1991, Donahue included seventy-five of his best stories in a collection titled *Terrifying Steamboat Stories,* published by Altwerger & Mandel Publishing Co.

Donahue collaborated with Judge James H. Lincoln, Harbor Beach, Michigan, in the book *Fiery Trial,* a historical account of a forest fire that swept the Thumb Area of Michigan in 1881. *Fiery Trial* was published by the Historical Society of Michigan in 1984. Anchor Publications reprinted a revised form of *Fiery Trial,* with the cooperation of the Historical Society, in 1994.

In 1982, Donahue and his wife, Doris, owned and used an old-time wood-burning cook stove in their home. They wrote and published *Cooking On Iron,* a collection of early American recipes ranging from Chestnut Soup and Hickory Nut Cake, to making soap. His story, *The Day We Wrecked the Train,* a personal account about growing up in Harbor Beach, appeared in a special edition of *Good Old Days Magazine* in 1987.

Other books by Donahue include *Schooners In Peril,* a collection of stories with pictures about disasters involving tall ships on the lakes, and *Steaming Through Smoke and Fire 1871,* a collection of true stories about shipwrecks and other events affecting lakers during the year 1871. *Steamboats in Ice 1872* is the second of a planned series of books examining events on the lakes during the same eventful decade.

James and Doris Donahue live near Cass City, Mich., with their daughter, Jennifer. The Donahues have three other children; Aaron, who lives with his wife, Gayle, in California, Ayn Bishop, of Georgia, and Susie Donahue, who lives in Germany.